This book is sweet, savory, spicy, and spiky all at the same time—a gentle masterpiece on the Jesus story that is breathtaking in its fresh insights and original voice.

LEONARD SWEET
Author, *From Tablet to Table*; professor; founder, preachthestory.com

Sneezing Jesus is inviting, compelling, revealing, instructive, hopeful, and inspiring. Brian's insights and arresting storytelling gave me fresh passion to worship Jesus and to participate in bringing His Kingdom to all those around me. What can I say, really, except that I love this book? I was changed in ways I long to be changed.

STASI ELDREDGE
Bestselling author, *Captivating* and *Becoming Myself*

Brian takes some well-worn and well-traveled Scripture and brings refreshing insights to it. Being truly human as a Christ follower means a much greater awareness of who really is within us. Allowing Him to infuse every moment with the consciousness of His presence changes us and those around us. This book is refreshing, stimulating, and challenging in our journey with Jesus and fellow believers.

REV. DR. HARRY L. THOMAS JR.
Cofounder, Creation Festivals

We tell our children, "You can be anything you want to be." But what if we told them, "Be like Jesus and you will be everything God made you to be"? *Sneezing Jesus* is an intriguing study of Jesus' life that reveals our purpose as believers.

DR. JOHN HULL
Lead pastor, Eastside Baptist Church, Marietta, GA; contributor, *100 Huntley Street*

Want to refresh your faith? *Sneezing Jesus* will cause you to gaze upon Jesus and see things you have never noticed before. This delightful portrait of our wonderful Savior is a joy to read. *Sneezing Jesus* caused me to fall deeper in love with Jesus.

TOM DOYLE
Author, *Standing in the Fire* and *Killing Christians*

It was so good for my heart to walk the human road that Jesus walked and absorb the intention of His humanity. A simple, beautiful portrayal of our intended relationship with the Divine.

ROBERT BEESON
Founder, Essential Records, iShine, and Solo Parent Society; former SVP, Sony/Provident; author, *Going Solo*

Few writers can put skin on God, making Him real and approachable. Brian is a master at allowing his reader to touch Jesus while at the same time instilling in them a deep reverence and awe for the creator of the universe. *Sneezing Jesus* is a must-read!

ADAM STADTMILLER
Pastor, La Jolla Christian Fellowship; author of *Praying for Your Elephant*

Sneezing Jesus opens our hearts and minds to the simple, powerful fact that Jesus has "been there, done that." This book will leave you wanting more, believing for more, and expecting more in your life with Jesus. I'll never look at sneezing the same again.

MARK RAMPULLA
Lead pastor, Southview Church, Spring Hill, TN

Sneezing Jesus will inspire Christians, whether leaders or church members, to walk intimately with our Lord. Discover how Jesus will redeem our individual humanity—flaws and all!

HARRY R. JACKSON JR.
Senior pastor, Hope Christian Church, Beltsville, MD; bishop, International Communion of Evangelical Churches

Trying to capture the humanity of Jesus while keeping clearly in view his divinity is no small feat, but *Sneezing Jesus* accomplishes that with rare clarity. Brian helps us grasp Jesus' humanity in a way that is both inspiring and vividly human.

DR. RAY MITSCH
Chair, Department of Psychology, Colorado Christian University

When heaven and earth meet, the boundary lines are indistinguishable. The collaboration between the divine and human are seamless in Jesus—and what our normal is supposed to be. I encourage you to grab this book.

DARREN TYLER
Conduit Mission founding president and lead pastor of Conduit Church

Sneezing Jesus

How God Redeems
Our Humanity

BRIAN HARDIN

A NavPress resource published in alliance
with Tyndale House Publishers, Inc.

NAVPRESS⊘®

NavPress is the publishing ministry of The Navigators, an international Christian organization and leader in personal spiritual development. NavPress is committed to helping people grow spiritually and enjoy lives of meaning and hope through personal and group resources that are biblically rooted, culturally relevant, and highly practical.

For more information, visit www.NavPress.com.

Sneezing Jesus: How God Redeems Our Humanity

Copyright © 2017 by Brian Hardin. All rights reserved.

A NavPress resource published in alliance with Tyndale House Publishers, Inc.

NAVPRESS and the NAVPRESS logo are registered trademarks of NavPress, The Navigators, Colorado Springs, CO. *TYNDALE* is a registered trademark of Tyndale House Publishers, Inc. Absence of ® in connection with marks of NavPress or other parties does not indicate an absence of registration of those marks.

The Team:
Don Pape, Publisher
Caitlyn Carlson, Acquisitions Editor
David Zimmerman, Copyeditor
Jennifer Phelps, Designer

Cover photograph of halo copyright © bernardojbp/Depositphotos. All rights reserved.

Unless otherwise indicated, all Scripture quotations are the author's paraphrase.

Scripture quotations marked KJV are taken from the *Holy Bible*, King James Version.

Scripture quotations marked NASB are taken from the New American Standard Bible,® copyright © 1960, 1962, 1963, 1968, 1971, 1972, 1973, 1975, 1977, 1995 by The Lockman Foundation. Used by permission.

Scripture quotations marked NIV are taken from the Holy Bible, *New International Version,*® *NIV.*® Copyright © 1973, 1978, 1984, 2011 by Biblica, Inc.® Used by permission. All rights reserved worldwide.

Scripture quotations marked NLT are taken from the *Holy Bible*, New Living Translation, copyright © 1996, 2004, 2015 by Tyndale House Foundation. Used by permission of Tyndale House Publishers, Inc., Carol Stream, Illinois 60188. All rights reserved.

Some of the anecdotal illustrations in this book are true to life and are included with the permission of the persons involved. All other illustrations are composites of real situations, and any resemblance to people living or dead is purely coincidental.

For information about special discounts for bulk purchases, please contact Tyndale House Publishers at csresponse@tyndale.com, or call 1-800-323-9400.

Cataloging-in-Publication Data is available.

ISBN 978-1-63146-740-0

Printed in the United States of America

23	22	21	20	19	18	17
7	6	5	4			

FOR JILL

Contents

00.

Prologue

On flesh and words

IF YOU WERE ASKED to describe Jesus using only one word, what would it be? Does such a word even exist?

Would it be Savior? God? Shepherd? Companion? Rabbi? Healer? Leader? Prophet? Carpenter? Son? Lamb? Teacher? Wise? Innocent? Obedient?

Honest?

Or maybe *real.* After all, Jesus was deeply tangible. He had a way of describing reality that was masterful and unsettling at the same time. Even today His words call Wisdom from the fringes and give her permission to dance in the sun. And Jesus consistently told people that how they perceived reality was not actually how things really were. He called out the plot behind the story and spoke to what was really going on behind the overlay of culture and fear. He spoke the language of the heart.

But still—He's so much more than even that, isn't He? I confess that boiling Jesus down into one word feels impossible. Much of this is because we each experience Jesus differently, depending on our own story of Him and our story with Him. For me, there really is only one word that describes my understanding of and relationship with Jesus—only one that snaps all others into place:

Human.

Jesus is the reality of God's desire to be included in the human story. It was an ache so deep and a love so vast that He was willing to step out of perfection and join the fray as a human being. Isn't that compelling? Jesus loved us enough to saddle Himself with indigestion and urination and all manner of humanness. He laughed with a human voice and saw through human eyes. In order to be Emmanuel—God *with* us—Jesus sneezed. He was one of us. And His very humanity tells us profound things about who *we* are, and about God's heart toward us in our humanity.

Much of the time, the part of Jesus' life we focus most on is His death. But He isn't just a means to an end. He isn't the cream we buy and apply twice a day to get rid of our sin rash. God didn't just come here to die and be resurrected. It didn't take Him thirty-three years to work up the courage to go to the cross. Most of what Jesus did had nothing to do with saving the world. He stayed among us a long time as one of us, and that time had a purpose. He came to show us what humanity is supposed to look like.

Which is interesting, isn't it? We spend a lot of our lives wanting to be anything but human, trying to be anywhere but here, and doing everything we can to de-flesh ourselves. We want to get out of this sin-infested cesspool and enter eternity with God, where we no longer have to struggle to live and behave. But Jesus' humanity teaches us something extraordinary: *Right now* is part of eternity. This sin-infested cesspool of humanity is our species. Right now matters. Being human matters.

Now, I am in no way attempting to diminish Jesus' divinity. Quite the contrary. If Jesus is not divine, the hope of eternity through Him is meaningless. But we often focus wholly on the divinity of Jesus while subtly diminishing His humanity. And this gives an incomplete picture of Jesus, in whom we see the human and the divine occupying the same space at the same time.[1] There is no evidence that Jesus' plan was to become the caricature of a supernatural superperson. What we find in Jesus' humanity is less about supernatural ability and more about normal humanity. In living with humans as a human, Jesus was showing us what it's supposed to look like to be people: people who are fully alive, whole, and human—who are utterly dependent on and deeply intertwined with God.

What if we were to look at Jesus as the most normal human who ever lived? What if we realized that the process of sanctification—of being set apart, of becoming more like Jesus—doesn't mean escaping our humanity but rather becoming fully human again?

This book is my humble attempt to make the flesh become word—to help us see Jesus for who He was and is. This is the Jesus I know. These are some of the things I've learned from the human God. This is my love story, and the love story offered to us all. And together we're going to look at Jesus through the lens of the Gospels and explore the reality of His humanity and what it says about our own.

May we all be delighted and surprised at the beauty of the Savior. And may we all find in Jesus, the human God, just what life could be.

Advent

On brokenness and wholeness

*God's movement is often abrupt and
unsettling rather than predictable and settling.*

MICHAEL JOSEPH BROWN

LONG AGO, in a land far away, there was an unspoiled garden created for a special purpose: to cradle and nourish the
most captivating of God's creatures—humans. Among all
the intricate life born out of creation—the plants and the
insects, the birds and the beasts—these human creatures were
unique. They were God-like, crafted in the image of their
Creator. God had, indeed, breathed His own life into them,
offering them living souls.[1] And to these exquisite creatures,
God bequeathed the earth in all its elaborate wonder.

In this time, before time was being counted, these humans
lacked nothing. The world was without conflict. Everything
was in harmony. All was perfect and whole, as it was intended

to be. This essential state of being would later have a name: *shalom*. God's peace and order were perfect in all places, at all times, and in all things. Wholeness was completely normal.

Upon these human creatures, God bestowed incredible abilities. In collaboration with their Creator Father, they could in turn create other life after God's image. God also gave them the gift of a will, one of the most powerful of all gifts, which allowed them the choice to enter into relationship with their Creator—the essence of true love. And true love it was.

These human creatures were a seamless and perfect transition between the physical and the spiritual. They could at once be present in their humanness and commune with their Creator in spirit. The soul of the divine and the physicality of the human occupying the same space at the same time was, like shalom, completely normal. God was within them and around them, and they knew and experienced nothing but perfection.

Unfortunately, it was not to last.

Among the swaying grass and intricate forestry of the garden, God placed two specific trees. One became known as the tree of life, and God's children were invited to eat their fill of its fruit and enjoy life eternal. The other tree was known as the tree of the knowledge of good and evil. This one was forbidden. In all of creation, the fruit of this tree was the one thing God asked His children not to partake of.

Although the Creator had prohibited His children from eating this fruit, He did not take away their ability to choose otherwise. Love isn't love if there's no way out. And allowing this choice created a vulnerability. After all, loving and collaborative relationships require this kind of trust.

A time came when the first man and woman found themselves before the tree of the knowledge of good and evil, absorbing a deception that would bring devastating results. Satan told them that if they ate the fruit dangling before them, they would become like God. In perhaps the cosmic irony of all time, they had somehow forgotten that they already were.

And so they ate. The juice of rebellion that flowed into their bodies was fatal to their souls. A breach was opened. Trust was broken. The misused gift of will and choice shattered the intimate love and trust between Creator and created. With one decision, humankind created a new reality for itself—one that had never been intended, one that fractured humanity at its core. No longer were humanity and divinity intertwined in a state of shalom. Eden had fallen.

Armed with the knowledge of good and evil but separated from divinity, humans forged their way forward, only to systematically discover their powerlessness. Hate was born. Conflict was created. Murder was committed. Death was introduced.

As humankind tried to find its way back to shalom on its own terms, the consequences of the breach between the human and the divine became more and more apparent: Humanity had fallen into inhumanity.[2] They had become subhuman, like animals, separated from God. The human soul was empty. Every attempt to fill the void created further devastation on a planet meant to be filled with the unfiltered glory of the Creator. Humanity became entombed in its own knowledge of good and evil. But the knowledge could not lead it back to its Creator, and so humanity began to forget who it was. All was lost.

And yet—the Creator Father had not abandoned them. He was waiting, watching, preparing to redeem the whole devolved mess. But a rescue would require something daring, painful, and unspeakably vulnerable. One day, at the precise moment of His choosing, God would invade the earth to rescue a species He had fashioned in His own image—an image He would not surrender to the darkness. And the invasion would be so counterintuitive, most wouldn't even understand what had happened until the victory was already won.

And that's what brings us to Jesus.

Mary was about fifteen years old, and she was engaged to be married. On this day, a day like any other, she had much to contemplate: leaving home, joining a new family, creating a new home, having sex for the first time, becoming a woman. But she had no idea that her world—and the human story itself—was about to change.

"Hello, favored woman. The Lord is with you."

The speaker's name was Gabriel. He was a chief among the angels of God.

Mary, startled from her daydream, couldn't figure out

what this strange man was trying to say—or who he was. To reassure her, Gabriel began to state his business.

"Don't be afraid, Mary, for you have found favor with God. I have great news! You're going to be a mother! The baby will be a boy, and you will name Him Jesus. He'll be a King! He'll be known as the Son of God, and His Kingdom will never end!"

Mary's blank stare revealed her confusion. Was he talking about the children she would have with her beloved Joseph? He must be. But who was this stranger? What if someone saw her talking to him? It was highly irregular for her to be approached by a man who wasn't in her family—and this man was saying crazy things. What was going on?

Stepping back, she stammered out the first words she could think of: "How? I'm a virgin."

When Gabriel spoke again, something shifted inside Mary. Curiosity began to rise up in her. What if this really was an angel of God? Either she had lost her mind—or she was truly being visited by Heaven.

"The Holy Spirit will come upon you," Gabriel said, "and the Most High will overshadow you. So the baby to be born will be holy, and he will be called the Son of God."

He then spoke about her cousin Elizabeth. Mary was taken aback. How could he know Elizabeth was part of her family? How could he know about Elizabeth's miraculous pregnancy? Could what he said be for real? And what could she do? All her life she'd loved God. And if this angel was from Him—he must be from Him!—and God was asking this of her, Mary, who was no one special from nowhere special . . . how could she say no?

The words spilled from her lips before she could catch them. "I am the Lord's servant," she said. And then, words that resonated from the center of her soul—"May everything you've said come true."

And the angel was gone.

Mary slowly turned, looking for Gabriel, listening for his voice, but heard only the light breeze. The conversation had lasted but a minute. And while the world looked the same, everything had changed.

Imagine that first minute. Imagine that young peasant girl standing alone, the only human being in the world who knew anything had happened. This was how counterintuitively the Creator chose to invade the world.

The thoughts twisting and rolling in her mind must have been overwhelming. She had agreed to the most preposterous thing she'd ever heard. She had become vulnerable in a way that would alter the trajectories of everyone she loved. She did trust in the Lord and had offered herself with her whole heart—but trust was all that she had to hold on to. She wasn't sure what had just happened.

The world began to spin. She could feel herself teetering when two thoughts brought her back to her senses:

What am I going to tell my father?

What am I going to tell Joseph?

For days those questions consumed her. She needed to tell someone, but what if her story proved untrue? She would be

punished severely for such a completely outrageous prank—
or worse, she would be considered mentally unhinged. She
battled between believing she'd been visited by an actual
angel . . . and fearing she'd lost her senses.

The conversations, when they finally came, must have
been awful. If my beautiful daughter told me she was unexpectedly pregnant, with the caveat that she'd not had sex at
all and the father was actually God, I would have no small
amount of skepticism. I would need an angel experience of
my own.

And no one believed Mary at first. Joseph was
brokenhearted—but he still loved her. He began considering
plausible ways to keep the matter quiet, to avoid humiliating
Mary publicly and destroying her and her family. At the same
time, Mary was spirited out of town as quickly as possible,
sent off to the hill country to visit Elizabeth. Mary hoped
that visiting Cousin Elizabeth would be the breath of grace
that she needed. And it was.[3]

But then, back in Galilee, everything changed. Amid
heartache and betrayal, an angel went to Joseph in a dream—
and Joseph was invited into the story in a rush of grace. The
angel told Joseph that Mary was pure and true, that this baby
was truly from God and of God. Mary was to be Joseph's
wife, and Joseph was to name the baby boy Jesus. And this is
what he would do as soon as Mary returned from the south.

Mary returned home during her second trimester. The
adjustment was awkward at first, but everyone managed.
Those who didn't believe Mary kept it to themselves. After

all, Joseph was sticking by Mary, so what else was there to say? It wasn't the grand celebration that had been planned, but this was the best possible solution. Joseph and Elizabeth appear to be the only ones who believed Mary's story without reservation. So as the months went by, Mary grew a thick skin along with her expanding midsection. The baby was kicking now, and Mary was amazed and in love.

The announcement that everyone would be required to migrate to their ancestral homes for a census couldn't have come at a more inconvenient time. The baby was expected any day, but Joseph couldn't refuse to participate in the census. Much of his livelihood came from the Romans. And people knew him—he was a respected artisan with skills in both wood and stone. He couldn't just disappear. But he couldn't leave Mary either.

He led their colt out of Nazareth; Mary rode on its back with a couple of extra blankets to cushion her. An agile and light traveler could make the journey in about four days, but Joseph and Mary were neither agile nor light. Joseph worried about how and where the baby would be born—because the baby was certain to come before they made the journey back. When they finally tottered into Bethlehem, dusty and weary, all they wanted was something to eat and a place to sleep. Unfortunately, as the Bible puts it, "there was no room for them in the inn."[4]

The hospitality business was booming, thanks to the census. It seemed as though everyone in the entire province had been displaced. No matter how much Joseph begged for shelter for a very pregnant woman, there simply was nowhere to stay. Finally, one man took compassion on them: They could stay in his stable, which was a cave where animals were kept. Joseph and Mary were grateful to have a place to lie down. The cave wasn't so bad. And at least they'd made it to Bethlehem.

Joseph was talking about whether to leave Mary for a short excursion to find food when she felt the first real contraction. It tightened like a belt around her waist and radiated deep into her back. She held her breath until she finally had to cry out. She locked eyes with Joseph. The baby was coming.

Joseph unloaded their belongings and set about attempting to make the place slightly more sanitary. Mary tried to get comfortable, which was difficult on a dirt floor in an open cave filled with animals. But the animals cooperated. They knew instinctively that new life was coming.

And it did.

Before the night was over, the shrieking of Mary gave way to the tiny whimper of a newborn baby boy. In the most normal of ways, God had come to be with us.

This is how Jesus became a human being. This is how the Creator Father chose to become a person and dwell among us. It's how the prophecy of Immanuel moved from a concept into a reality. And while this tells us much about God's heart toward people, it also tells us much about ourselves.

If this were our story to tell, we would have imagined God

arriving a little higher up the food chain, in full adulthood and total competency. It would make sense for Him to skip the messiness of infancy, the awkwardness of childhood. It would make more sense for Him to come to earth as royalty. But this is precisely what God didn't do. And this is the first clue that God's view of humanity is different from our own. Jesus would proclaim this message relentlessly throughout His ministry.

We shouldn't overlook this. God chose to slide through a birth canal and come helpless, naked, and screaming into the world like any other human baby—completely vulnerable. He wasn't born potty-trained. He had to have His bottom wiped. He probably peed on His mommy more than once. He suckled at her breast in order to be nourished. He had to grow in strength and learn balance before He could take His first steps. He took no shortcuts. In every way He was a human being. And that is the point. He was perfect, and perfectly normal. He was a human as humanity was intended all the way back in the Garden.

God chose to fully become one of us in every respect,[5] and He came in a way that was baffling and unsettling. His coming twisted so many cultural norms out of shape—and perhaps it should similarly challenge us. God, who could have come to Earth in any way He wanted, chose to come as a peasant to a place few knew of. God chose to be ordinary.

Jesus was born into a family, and He grew up in the context of human relationships. He had a keen sense of the people around Him and their connection to the earth that provided their home. He understood the bond between parents and children. He learned all the things children discover as they mature. He learned to work with wood and stone alongside Joseph—to get into the soil, craft with His hands, and create things. Creating was—and is—His nature. Relationship was—and is—His nature. And these things are the essence of what we are made of.[6]

But Jesus did more than identify with and embody our humanity—His very human arrival revealed the extent of humankind's loss of identity. After all, God arrived through the scandal of an unwed pregnancy. He was born into relative poverty and total obscurity. Before He could talk, He was a homeless refugee. In all of humanity, there seemed to be no place for the Creator in whose image humans were made.

Our humanity was fractured long ago in a garden. At the Fall, we actually fell. We slid downward and backward away from the way we were created to be. We were never supposed to be separated from God. And the effects of this separation aren't hard to miss in the world—which is to say that it's not hard to see how far we have fallen.

And this is why Jesus' arrival, the ordinary moments and details of His coming, are so important. Because although we look at Jesus' arrival as an extraordinary event—and yes, the very fact that God came at all is *extraordinary*—we can't forget the radical importance of the ordinary. That perhaps Jesus' human life was more about what ordinary humanity was supposed to look like—that His life was largely spent reminding His creation what they were supposed to be from the start.

02.

Backward

On utter dependence and kingdoms

In seclusion, she had secluded herself from a thousand
natural and healing influences; that, her mind, brooding
solitary, had grown diseased, as all minds do and must and
will that reverse the appointed order of their Maker.

CHARLES DICKENS, *Great Expectations*

I ONCE DRESSED MYSELF, drove to the airport, went through the entire security process, flew to another city, attended and spoke at an event, and finally found my way to a hotel room late in the evening before realizing that I'd been wearing my shirt inside out the entire time. Granted, it was a T-shirt, but throughout the entire day no one had casually mentioned the mistake to me. I felt a bizarre mixture of retro-embarrassment and disbelief that no one had pointed it out.

When we get down to it, our whole world is inside out, and humanity in general is completely unaware. But our utterly wonderful Jesus came to reverse all of that.

In the Gospels, Jesus' words often have an urgent, almost perplexed quality to them. He is profoundly patient and compassionate, but at times He is exasperated. The larger narrative that seems to hover over everything about Jesus, as I read it, is that we've got life inside out. We're living backward from how life is supposed to be, and our expectations are completely out of sync with how things really are.

Take, for example, the Sermon on the Mount—perhaps the centerpiece of Jesus' teachings.[1]

Jesus was speaking to people who felt repressed and disrespected. They hung on His words because He spoke their language. He was one of them. He knew this repression and disrespect intimately as a fellow Hebrew and a fellow human.

In their mind-set, a person who was punched needed to be willing to punch back twice as hard. This was the way to acquire respect—through strength and resistance. And life had punched these folks plenty. The Galileans were known for their penchant for insurrection. They were squarely on the Roman radar. And these people wanted a liberator—a godly leader full of charisma who could rally them all together to revolt and throw off the Roman occupation and oppression. This constricting sense of persecution was a low and simmering slice of their culture.

To these people—as is still often the case today—the ideas of accepting things as they were, or being merciful to an enemy, or actively making peace instead of being the resistance, were, for the most part, fantasy concepts. Sure, they'd be nice if they were possible, but they were hardly realistic.

This is why Jesus' words that day on a lovely rise overlooking the Sea of Galilee were both illuminating and alarming. Jesus called to something deeper in the people listening—something more true and whole:

"You're lucky if you're poor and empty right now—the Kingdom of Heaven is yours. You're fortunate if you're mourning now because you have comfort to look forward to. Those of you who actively accept the unpleasantness around you are blessed. It won't always be this way. You will inherit the earth. You're blessed if you crave righteousness. That craving will be satisfied."[2]

Jesus articulated nine different affirmations comprising nine disruptive juxtapositions. In just a few short moments He had everyone's full attention. He was weaving a completely different reality from anything they'd ever experienced—and in profoundly connected ways, different from anything *we* have ever experienced. Jesus flipped everything on its side, at once both magnifying the world the people wanted to live in and showing them the one they had created. Jesus described the flow and posture of human life as it was intended—the deep exhale and utter relief of total dependence on God.

It's as if Jesus were saying, "You've got it inside out. The way you were made to live is opposite from the way you're living. You are the salt of the earth. You are the light of the world. But you're living backward, and it's not working."

Then he described what life should look like, what normal humans should be like, and in the process He raised the bar on the Mosaic law:

"You've got to be more righteous than your religious leaders.[3] Everyone knows they will be brought to justice if they murder someone, but the underlying rage is just as big of a problem. If someone has something against you, go and reconcile, even if you're at the altar before God."[4]

On and on He touched every soft spot of life and raised expectations. But was He only dishing out more rules no one can achieve? Or was our inability to achieve them actually the point?

The reality of how much mercy we require each day and how much grace we're consuming to live is astonishing. We cannot live independent from God. Separation from Him lowers us to our basest animal selves and disconnects us from what we were created for. Utter dependence on God is supposed to be our normal reality.

Jesus described a spacious life with vast reservoirs of unity and opportunity and a clear heart. One in which nothing comes between us and anyone else—no anger, no racial tension, no misunderstanding, no war. This kind of life transcends mere action or raw discipline. It goes beyond all of that to what is really going on inside us—what our true motives are. And we can't look away because what Jesus was describing was shalom: the wholeness we long for.

And what of this Kingdom Jesus continually referred to? He talked about it everywhere. His Kingdom language was what caused people to wonder if He was the Messiah they were hoping for—the liberator who would bring freedom. His Kingdom language still stirs our hearts today.

But His Kingdom language seems to describe something completely different from what the people expected. The Kingdom they'd imagined and longed for was one in which a Messiah would emerge and gather the true. They would overthrow their occupiers and establish their own sovereign rule under God. Jesus' description of the Kingdom set their hearts on fire, but they interpreted His words through the lens of their worldview—as we still do today.

"Seek first the Kingdom of God and His righteousness, and all these things will be added to you"[5] wasn't a battle cry. It was an invitation to live whole.

"The Kingdom of Heaven is at hand"[6] wasn't a summons to attack. It was an offer to see what was already among them.

Over and over Jesus attempted to awaken His listeners to the fact that the Kingdom wasn't going to be what they'd imagined. It had already begun and was already there. The way they were envisioning it was completely inside out.

It's like a man who sows good seed in a field.[7] It's like a tiny mustard seed that is seemingly insignificant but grows and becomes strong.[8] It's like leaven that is mixed in with flour.[9] It's like treasure hidden in a field.[10] It's like a merchant in search of fine pearls.[11] It's like a net that is thrown into the sea and gathers fish of every kind.[12] It's like a king who gives a wedding feast for his son.[13]

Continually, Jesus described the Kingdom in terms that one can't point to and identify specifically—but in every story, the Kingdom was the essential piece. The Kingdom is mixed in and present already. It's like leaven in a loaf of bread.

A person can't find the leaven after the loaf is baked. But the loaf would be completely deflated and radically different if the leaven were missing. The Kingdom is like a tiny mustard seed that sprouts into a giant bush. Someone couldn't find the original mustard seed after the bush has grown, but birds could not nest in the branches were it not for the seed.

"The Kingdom of God is not coming in ways that you can observe," Jesus said. "No one will be able to say, 'Look, here it is,' or 'It's over there.' The Kingdom of God is already within and among you."[14]

These words are such a colossal paradigm shift—an upside-down way of looking at an inside-out world. And they are as disruptive now as when they were spoken. Jesus was telling the people then (and us now) that we won't be able to identify the Kingdom geographically or point it out in any one singular event. Even though the fullness of the Kingdom is not yet realized, the Kingdom has already begun, and we are a vital part of that realization. It's everywhere—and it's now. It is within us and among us and worth losing all we have to gain it.

We are to be actively involved in this Kingdom, right now, in the midst of our humanness. Otherwise we're completely ignoring our reality while waiting for something that isn't going to happen. We have a massive and collaborative role to play. We are invited into the story, and everywhere we go we have the chance to invite and establish the Kingdom. And we're supposed to do it in the most counterintuitive of ways—we're supposed to truly love one another.

This is not just a concept or metaphor. We're supposed to actively love as a direct response to offense. It's not a weak posture—it's a strong and aggressive one. To actively engage with one who has burdened us with insult or transgression, and to vigorously go the extra mile to find a path toward radical reconciliation—to turn the other cheek—is strong, courageous, and noble. This kind of response is supposed to be normal—our first instinct. And it can be . . . but only if we're wholly dependent on God. Jesus' beautiful dismantling of a complex, generationally ingrained way of life, and His reconstruction of a picture of humanity's true form, is breathtaking.

Can you imagine a world where everyone always turned the other cheek? How could there possibly be misunderstanding that leads to conflict? There would never be an event that escalated to war, whether in a relationship or between nations. And this kind of humanity is accessible. We've got to stop living backward. All throughout history we can see what humanity looks like when we try to be our own god—what we are capable of in our own strength. Utter dependence on God removes impossibilities and the need to struggle with one another, because nothing is impossible with God.[15]

My little son doesn't know anything is impossible yet. He thinks I'm Superman. He's absolutely convinced I have magical powers. Every day is full of vivid discovery. Jesus said, "Truly I tell you, anyone who will not receive the kingdom of God like a little child will never enter it."[16]

My son is the kind of child Jesus was referring to. He

depends on me for life. He instinctively knows that I'll protect him. In fact, he doesn't want to be too far away from his mother or me because he knows who we are, and he knows he's safe in our presence. He doesn't believe there's anything we can't do. And he doesn't believe there's much of anything he can't do either. Doesn't this perfectly describe the way Jesus invites us to live as normal human beings?

Jesus taught us to be utterly dependent on God; grateful for the gift of life, intimacy, and collaboration; profoundly thankful that we're not all alone on this planet. We have our brothers and sisters, and they are also created in God's image. Together we make up a whole—a body. Our ideology may have its nuances, but we are the Kingdom and it is now. We're the ones advancing or retreating.

What if we lost one month from the grand total of our earthly lives every time we spoke words of death and darkness into the world or acted in a way that is inhumane? We'd pay attention then, wouldn't we?

If we could begin to take Jesus at His word and live what He taught us, the human story could radically change—the loaf would rise, the mustard seed would grow. Together we make up the body of Christ and the Kingdom of God in this world. If we could see ourselves the way Jesus sees us, everything could change. Jesus isn't the holdup. We are. We must live believing, as my son does, that anything is possible.

Jesus wasn't only offering aspirations for a more pleasing life—He was inviting us to stop living in an inside-out world, to rise up and become who we were created to be: truly human people who reflect the glory of the Lord throughout the earth.[17] Let us answer this invitation and love God with all our hearts, minds, and strength—and love one another as we love ourselves.[18] And as we turn away from our lowest selves, may we utterly depend on God and hear the echo of Jesus' words calling to us across time: "Fear not, little flock; for it is your Father's good pleasure to give you the kingdom."[19]

03

Weep

On tear bottles and pour-overs

Tears come from the heart and not from the brain.

LEONARDO DA VINCI

IT'S REMARKABLE the kinds of things we learn from the very start. In normal human development, babies understand early on that crying will bring someone running. As soon as babies' little tear ducts are developed enough, tears overflow and trickle down their cheeks—whether for want of food or comfort or sleep. Babies have no problem releasing what they cannot hold inside. They naturally let it go—and a parent comes quickly. And even as adults, we understand the enormous power in these little salty droplets that seep from our eyes.

When I think about tears, I think about Luke 7. It's a well-known story: A woman with an alabaster jar of expensive ointment seeks out Jesus and weeps at His feet. But what we can easily miss is this woman's courage to face ridicule and scorn in order to withhold nothing from her God.

Jesus had become a bit of a religious celebrity, and the spiritual leaders of the day were trying Him on for size and deciding what they thought about Him. He'd been invited to one of their homes for a dinner party, and somehow the woman in question found out about it. She wasn't the type of person who would ordinarily be invited anywhere near that kind of event, but she took a risk and snuck in uninvited.

The mere sight of Jesus moved her to tears. Lowering her head, she slid along the wall, trying to remain invisible as she worked her way around the room and knelt behind Jesus. She couldn't face him. It must have been the strangest sensation for Jesus as tiny kisses began to caress His feet unexpectedly.

Touching the rabbi at all was unorthodox, but this was beyond the pale. For Jesus to allow this in public was highly sensual and unconventional at best—especially from a woman who had a questionable history. It wouldn't be any less odd now. This wasn't just happening in public either. It was happening in the home of a spiritual leader and would have caused the guests to have second thoughts about Jesus' reputation. But He allowed it, caring little for what people might have thought about Him. He navigated this awkward situation the way He navigated all of His life: He looked behind the façade of culture and social hierarchy and saw what was true and unsuppressed.

Tears traced their way down the woman's dusty cheeks and dripped onto His feet as she kissed them. The well of this woman's sorrow was obviously deep and filled with regret. She was crying so hard that she needed to use her long black hair as a towel to wipe His feet.

I've always found this story a bit odd because, while I've seen people overwhelmed with emotion many times, I've never seen someone weep so profusely that they needed an actual towel to clean up. The entire scene is uncomfortable. It's scandalous, and yet its texture is rich and full of beautiful, heartbreaking humanity.

Tears are fascinating. They're a familiar part of life, and yet they sneak up on us when we're overcome by emotion, don't they? Tears speak in a language of honesty that transcends words. They uncover what's really going on in the depths of our hearts whether we like it or not—a wordless overflow that demands release and cannot be held back.

Somewhere in the shifting sands of culture we've reached a point where tears have become a negative social trigger. We're subtly taught to hold them back. Public weeping is often seen as fragility. If a man cries in public, some perceive him as weak. When a woman cries, her girlfriends are quick to dig through their handbags to find a tissue to wipe the tears away. And there's more to it than just salvaging mascara. Usually a person who openly weeps feels obligated to apologize for the discomfort his or her emotion evokes. Tears are wiped away and the tissues thrown into the wastebasket as soon as possible. For some reason, we think tears need to be tossed away along with the weakness they may represent. They make us feel as if we've lost control of ourselves.

There is deep irony in this. Our attempts to hide our tears are our own denial of what is really going on in our hearts, and this is a harsh diminishment of the beautiful gift of release. In withholding the truth of our human emotions, we are simply creating the illusion that we are in control— when we're not. The life of Jesus shows us that there is something sacred and beautifully human in releasing our grip and offering up our true emotions. Why do we withhold what is true and then try to create an illusion of control when Jesus lived and honored a different way?

In the first century, in the culture Jesus stepped into, women actually collected their tears, using tiny ornamental vases called tear bottles. Thousands of these bottles made from Roman glass have been discovered in archaeological sites throughout the ancient Roman Empire, and although expensive, they can be purchased from antiquities dealers today. Using a tear bottle was certainly a Roman custom, but it was also Jewish. Tear bottles are spoken of in the Psalms.[1]

A tear bottle is a simple enough contraption. It has a wide brim that narrows to a little tube opening into a tiny reservoir at the bottom. Women held on to their tears to reveal their grief, remorse, sadness, joy, love—all the deep and true emotions of humanity. In wartime, the tears collected would be given to a husband returning from war, a visual representation of how much he'd been missed and how much his wife had worried over him. Jesus inhabited a culture where tears were given value, embodying the highest and lowest points of life. Tears represented the moments so overpowering that the only response was the silent, visible truth of tremendous emotion.

This little cultural nuance explains a lot when it comes to the story of the woman who wept as she caressed and kissed Jesus' feet. She was obviously moved by Jesus. He may have been the only safe place for her to lay down what she had been trying to hold within. And in His presence she found her eyes spilling over with emotion. She brought with her what was most costly and valuable to her—the alabaster jar of ointment—and as she massaged the balm onto His feet, it certainly mixed with the tears flowing down her cheeks. But she had also probably brought a tiny vase full of the most bitter and painful regrets in her life. And it was upon His feet that she poured out all that had been collected and kept secret. She gave Jesus the pain of her life as an offering and then dried His feet with her hair—and Jesus let her do it because she was withholding nothing from Him. Social scandal aside, this was a true and truly human exchange.

Jesus entered into the scandalous scene with her and practically dared anyone to say anything. He wasn't unnerved at all. He was profoundly present to the woman, while totally aware of all the social rules being broken.

The evening's host, of course, reacted differently. The meaning of the entire prickly situation was lost on the religious leader who'd invited Jesus to dinner. He knew of this woman. He knew where she'd been, and he judged Jesus for it.

If this man were a legitimate prophet, He would know the kind of woman He is letting touch Him, he thought.[2]

But Jesus knew. He knew that her story went far deeper than her reputation—and He knew that she was offering Him all the pain of it, all the truth, holding nothing back. And as she knelt behind Him, kissing His feet and anointing them with her regret and suffering, He spoke up for her. He explained what she was doing, and then He did something even more scandalous than what she had been doing. As her tears crept down her cheeks, pooling and dripping from her chin, He stared beyond the well of her eyes and into her soul and said, "Your sins are forgiven."[3]

She had withheld nothing. She had, in fact, risked everything, bringing her most costly possession and her entire life story and offering both to Jesus, not knowing how He might respond. But Jesus responded with human touch and divine intervention in a perfect example of humanity as it was intended to be. He blessed her offering. He entered into her pain. He honored the truth behind her tears. He forgave.

What a release this must have been for her. As the bitterness of her life dripped from Jesus' feet, the sorrow in her eyes must have become joy. The murmurs of scandal and blasphemy in the room must have seemed a universe away as hope invaded her heart, washing it clean.

We bottle up a lot of things. We bottle them up inside rather than letting them out. We hide our brokenness, shoving it down and forcing it into the closets and basements of our hearts. We listen to the critical voice inside that reminds us of where we've been and how weak we are. We're afraid to be broken. We're even more afraid that we'll be exposed or lose control of ourselves.

Jesus was (and is) unruffled by this. Most of what we're trying to suppress is rooted in the fear of what others may think of us. Jesus didn't live this way. Jesus was interested in what was really going on, not in the fabrication of the false realities humankind creates for itself.

What soft spots in you would bring you to tears if you were to allow yourself to enter into them? The woman in this story held nothing back and risked everything to pour her life out before Jesus.

To be truly human is to withhold nothing from God. He's not embarrassed. It's not awkward for Him. Tears are a direct line to our soul in both joy and pain, and they speak beyond what we know how to say.

I don't know of the chains that have wrapped themselves around your ankles. I don't know the regrets and suffering that cause you to soak your pillow at night. We each have our own pool of shame to draw from. But tears are not our weakness. They represent everything we've endured to get to where we are right now, and maybe they ultimately speak of a truth that nothing else can. And perhaps there is only one place where we can pour them out. May we bring what is most precious to us, as well as what has tortured us, to the feet of Jesus and pour those things out as the offering of our very lives to Him. And like this woman, may we leave them there. Our sins are forgiven.

04

Go Away

On storms, swine, and naked men

A traveler on foot in this country seems to be considered as a
sort of wild man or out-of-the way being, who is stared at,
pitied, suspected, and shunned by everybody that meets him.

KARL PHILIPP MORITZ

THE SUMMER BEFORE JUNIOR HIGH SCHOOL was filled with anticipation. I was excited to leave elementary school behind me. Junior high sounded so robust and adult. And I felt ready—with one caveat. Physical education class. The rumor was that we had to shower after each class . . . and that the showering process was communal. In other words, we had to get naked and take a shower with a bunch of other naked guys. Not cool.

I wasn't alone in my anxiety about this. In one heartfelt and vulnerable exchange, my best friend looked at his shoes and said, "Dude, don't be looking at me in the shower." To which I replied, "Dude, I'm only going to be looking at myself."

To this day, a naked man remains one of the last things I'd like to see. If a naked man were running toward me, arms flailing and everything else jangling close behind, I would be highly unnerved. But this was precisely what Jesus encountered as He prepared to dock in the land of the Gerasenes.[1]

Jesus had spent the previous day ministering to people. He was utterly exhausted. He couldn't humanly go on anymore. He told His disciples to get the boat prepared, and they had it ready quickly. They were fishermen, after all—experts on the water. Jesus instructed them to head for the other side, to the Gerasene people, and then He curled up in the back of the boat and went to sleep.

A storm was brewing. The disciples saw the signs. The Sea of Galilee is a low-lying lake—the lowest freshwater lake in the world. Winds sweep in from the Mediterranean and off the mountains of the Golan Heights in legendary fashion. Storms on the Galilee spin like a hurricane and terrify many an experienced fisherman. The disciples were just hoping to outrun this one.

Jesus was still asleep when the waves became violent. The lightning lit the shoreline in the beating rain, and the disciples realized how far they had yet to go. There was no way the boat could handle this kind of punishment much longer. They began to panic.

Quickly maneuvering to the back of the boat, they shook Jesus awake. "We're going to drown!" they yelled.

Jesus slowly opened His eyes. First He considered the severe rocking of the boat, then the violence of the storm. As

He looked into the sky, the rain pelted His face. He rose to His knees and opened His mouth.

"Quiet," He said. "Be still."

The weather obeyed. The winds receded as the tempest pulled into the sky high above them. Within a few minutes the storm was but a memory.

Jesus looked over at His friends with a nearly imperceptible grin on His face. They were wide-eyed and speechless.

"Why were you afraid?" He asked them. "Where's your faith?"

They looked at one another and then tentatively back at Jesus. Had that just happened?

"Who is this man?" they whispered back and forth. "Even the wind and water obey Him."

It was after all of this that they landed upon the shore and a naked man charged to greet them. He must have seemed an apparition after what they'd gone through.

As it turned out, the naked man actually lived there in the wild, and Jesus and the disciples were the ones trespassing— sort of. The man lived in the nearby burial caves.

He continued to sprint down the shoreline toward them, screaming. When he was within earshot, they could hear what he was saying: "WHY ARE YOU INT—"

"Come out of him," Jesus interrupted from the back of the boat.

The disciples spun to look at Jesus. The man stopped in his tracks.

"Why are you interfering with me?" the man asked. "Are

you here to torture me? Please don't torture me, Jesus, Son of the Most High God."

"What is your name?" Jesus asked.

"There is a Legion of us."

Jesus and the man stared at each other. There was no sound save the distant caws of gulls and the lap of the water on the shore. Lowering his eyes, the man spoke again.

"Send us into the pigs," he said. "Don't send us into the faraway pit. Let us go into the pigs."

Jesus glared at the man. Five heartbeats went by before He responded.

"Go," He said.

The naked man slumped to his knees, and seconds later the nearby herd of swine went insane. They squeaked and squealed like a circus of rusty hinges from hell before bolting for the cliffs. Down into the water they splashed one by one, eventually drowning.

The herdsmen were terrified. They hadn't been paying much attention, but they'd seen Jesus' boat float up and the crazy man talking to Him. Then they saw Jesus point in their direction, and their pigs had gone berserk. Terrified, they ran to get help in the nearby villages. The great Decapolis city of Hippos (Sussita) was just up the mountain.

Word spread, and people streamed like a flock off the mountain. They could see the bobbing swine in the distance. It looked like a land invasion of the devils they believed ruled the sea and stirred the waters.

As the people arrived at the shoreline, they could sense

the tingle in the air. Something had happened, all right. The man whom no one could bind with rope or chain and who howled among the graves was wearing clothes and sitting with a smile on his face, holding a coherent conversation with a group of men who had arrived by boat. This must somehow be connected to the entire herd of pigs bobbing silently down the shore.

When the herdsmen returned and began telling the story, it became clear that the leader of the men in the boat had somehow cast a demon out of their resident madman and into the swine, who had then rushed to their own watery deaths.

A wave of astonishment passed through the crowd, followed by a wave of fear. There was no way to make sense of it. At first they pleaded with Jesus to leave them, then they insisted. They were afraid of what they were seeing.

Realizing that there was nothing left to be done on this visit, Jesus climbed back into the boat. His friends followed and prepared to launch. The man who had been delivered begged to leave with them, but Jesus invited him to return to his own life.

"Go back to your family." Jesus smiled, squeezing his shoulder. "Tell them all that God has done for you."

As they drifted away, the crowd noisily followed the man to his home. His story would become legendary as he told it throughout the villages.

The spot on which this encounter took place is now called Kursi. It sits on the northeastern shore of the Sea of Galilee, near the modern-day border with Jordan. It is the only place on the lake where cliffs snake their way down to the water. Ruins from a fifth-century Byzantine monastery stand as a memorial. On the hillside are ancient caves and burial sites as well as timeworn mosaic flooring from former shrines. In the springtime a golden sea of wild mustard flowers sways in the breeze, creating wave after wave of shimmering life.

I've stood on that spot a number of times, playing the story in my mind. It's compelling that Jesus would cross the lake and go through the storm for just one person. The confrontation is incredibly dramatic. But the thing that stops me in my tracks is the reaction of the people.

They asked Jesus to leave.

They had borne witness to a person being set free from demons. It was a demonstration of power and authority the likes of which they had never seen.

And their response was to ask Him to leave?

What catches me is that I've done this. I do this in so many ways. I've felt the presence of Jesus in a situation or relationship and shied away out of fear of what sort of involvement He might want from me. Or I've sensed God on the move in my life and wanted to control the outcome and govern the pace. I've watched God at work in the lives of others in ways that messed with my tidy box of assumptions or theology, and I've backed away. I've asked Him to leave too—in thought, word, and deed, by what I've done and by what I've left undone. I've become like a wide-eyed, speechless follower on a boat: I see the upward twitch of His mouth as He asks, "What are you so afraid of? Where is your faith?"

Who are we in this story? Are we running toward Jesus, broken and naked? Or are we, in fear, asking Him to leave? What are the thoughts, words, and deeds of our lives saying? Could it be that we're asking the One we need most to back off and then acting fearful and abandoned when He doesn't seem to be around? Are we saying that we really need His involvement, but trying to control and manage what it's going to look like through the choices we make each day?

In our own way, we all go to Jesus like the naked man. Left to our own plans and untethered from anything that connects us to God, we're all flailing naked people asking, "Why are you interfering with me?" We often misinterpret the disruptive ways of God in our lives. We want to define what is best for us—but the disruption is less about messing with our personal comfort and more about handing us our freedom.

So what are we afraid of?

Jesus couldn't have ordered a storm to calm down or thrown a legion of devils into a herd of swine if He didn't know He had the authority and power to make it happen. He knew His Father's command of things. And He knew He had been granted this authority as a human being. But was this miracle a once-in-a-lifetime event? Or was Jesus demonstrating what was supposed to be normal?

If Jesus was a perfect person—a perfect human being—and His sacrifice is what liberated and restored us to our intended humanity, then the way He lived His human life is precisely the way we are to live ours. Jesus was always aware of whatever situation He was facing and could interpret and navigate with a confidence and authority rarely seen. This same sort of authority is all throughout the New Testament.[2] And it's an authority that we apparently have. The Father's authority was given to Jesus, and Jesus bestowed it upon us. Jesus is within us. The divine is within our humanity.

So where is our faith? Do we functionally relegate this divine authority within us to a theological concept rather than living into it as essence and fact?

Those of us who follow Jesus have been given our Father's command of things. His goodness is unstoppable, and we get to live in the middle of it as sons and daughters. Let's not only bear witness to God's goodness, but be enveloped by it and participate in it. This is what it looks like to be Christ-like. This is what our normal is supposed to be. We must allow the authority of Jesus its rightful place in our lives and stop asking Him to leave by choosing our lowest selves—the less-than-human selves we were without God.

The only way we can live out God's authority in our everyday lives is if we truly embrace the fact that the Spirit of God is within us—for real. God is a part of who we are. The Scriptures tell us plainly that Christ lives within us[3] and that we are participants in the divine nature of God.[4] The old, devolved creature we once were without God is no longer supposed to be our reality. God created true humanity to be intertwined with Him.

Jesus redeemed our hopeless inhuman state and restored the way we were created to be. We are intimately interwoven with God in a collaboration we call life. God's Spirit and authority are available and, in fact, inseparable from our identity. We are sons and daughters of the Highest God and are a part of His ongoing redemptive work of sanctification in the world.

But this doesn't just happen. We can choose not to participate. Our choices are speaking volumes about this. Our lives are telling the story of whether we believe and are participating in this divine collaboration. Our lives either ask, "Why are you interfering with me?" or they invite God's interruption of everything that pulls us toward inhumanity. May we always remain intertwined and collaborating with Jesus in His work in the world—the business of awakening a slumbering species and setting free those who are naked and flailing.

05

Between a Place & a Hard Rock

On assumptions and the most important question

[People] have the unique ability to listen to
one story and understand another.

PANDORA POIKILOS, *Excuse Me, My Brains Have Stepped Out*

SEVERAL YEARS AGO, my wife, Jill, and I were in San
Francisco, shooting photographs for one of her music albums.
Jill would hop in the backseat and make wardrobe changes in
our rented vehicle as we moved about the city, which helped
us shoot in multiple locations while sticking to a shoestring
budget. As if by magic, she could disrobe, re-robe, and adjust
her makeup inconspicuously while I scouted shooting angles.

While searching for a view of the city skyline to use as
a backdrop, we wandered onto Yerba Buena Island, where
Jill promptly hopped in the backseat to do her magic and I
hopped out of the car to scout. Minutes later she emerged in
a lovely zebra-print dress.

I maneuvered her into several different angles in search of the most flattering light. She smiled, her cinnamon hair flowing with the breeze. We were both completely oblivious to the young man watching us.

After several minutes, he quietly approached and asked me if we were perhaps shooting the cover for an adult film. I just stared at him, attempting to process what he had just asked. He then informed me, while looking at my wife, of his desire to break into the business.

A silent pause blossomed between us.

This was a new experience. It had never occurred to me to prepare for such a conversation.

The outfit my wife wore was flattering but not immodest, and she certainly wasn't striking suggestive poses. Nevertheless, he had somehow concluded that Jill was an adult-film actress and that I was a photographer with connections. I couldn't land on whether I should feel flattered or outraged—or both.

Thankfully, I was able to gather my wits enough to tell him that no, we were in fact shooting for musical packaging. He thanked me and asked if I might know how he could break into the adult film industry. I assured him that I had no connections in that field.

The assumptions we leap to about people are fascinating. Sometimes we can create entire realities, complete with backstories. We can take offense about things that do not even exist. Assumptions mean we're using our God-given creative energy to invent a reality that, even if it contains threads of truth, is rounded out with plausible fabrications. A false reality, in other words. Jesus never did this—ever. But He did muse on our inhuman penchant for assumption.

"Who do the crowds say that I am?" He asked. "What are they saying?"[1]

Jesus had led His friends north, about fifteen miles from the villages along the Sea of Galilee, where they spent most of their time. He needed a reprieve to enjoy communion with the Father and catch His breath. The city of Caesarea Philippi was nearby—a city famous for pagan cultic practices that might have made even an adult film actor blush. Rabbis wouldn't go there. Once again sidestepping tradition, Jesus did.

The cultic portion of Caesarea Philippi was framed and defined by an ominous cliff face that towered above the temples beneath. A spring gushed from a grotto carved by nature into sheer rock. The immense cliffs could be seen from afar and had been revered as a holy site dating back centuries before Jesus went there. In Jesus' time, the celebrated deity was Pan—the half-man, half-goat god of desolate places. Pan was thought to instill panic into enemies while watching over the fields and groves of the area. He was also believed to possess beguiling fertility powers, and peculiar rituals around this belief were practiced openly in his temple. Without getting into too much detail, some of these fertility ceremonies included goats to honor the half-man, half-goat god.

In earlier times, people worshiped Baal at the mouth of the cave. It was thought that Baal would enter and depart the underworld through the ominous fissure known by the locals as the gates of hell.

It's fascinating that Jesus would go to Caesarea Philippi at all. The conversation He was having with His friends was even more fascinating because it confronts us with a question that cannot go unanswered.

"What are people assuming about me?" Jesus asked them.

"Some think you're a resurrected John the Baptist or one of the ancient prophets of old," they replied.

"But what about you?" Jesus asked. "Who do you say that I am?"

This is perhaps the most important question in the life of a human being. Its answer shapes the trajectory and scope of one's entire human experience. This question cannot be truly answered with irony or assumption. We must answer it from the center of our soul and identity—from a place that is true.

In the conversation Jesus was having, the young and candid disciple Simon spoke up.

"You are the Messiah—the Son of the Living God," he said.

"You did not learn this from another person," Jesus told him. "My Father in Heaven blessed you with this understanding. You will be known as Peter, and upon this rock I will build my church, and the gates of hell will not prevail against it."

And thus the apostle Peter was formed.

Theologians have contemplated Jesus' nuanced response for a couple thousand years. It seems reasonably apparent that Jesus didn't accidentally go to Caesarea Philippi. His response to Peter was obviously rooted in the geography. In making a declaration about the gates of hell not prevailing against His church, Jesus was using the cliffs and cave before them to illustrate a point. But what was the point?

Many believed this was a declaration ordaining Peter as the primary leader of the coming church. Through him, the anointing of apostolic succession would pass to future generations.

Others have concluded that the confession of Peter, and not Peter himself, was important because Jesus asked, "Who do you *say* that I am?" Peter's acknowledgment of Jesus' divinity as the Son of God was the rock upon which the church is built and formed. When we declare Jesus as Lord, we also are built upon this rock.

It is also possible that Jesus was pronouncing something much more daring.

Caesarea Philippi was notoriously degenerate in the eyes of religious Jews. It was considered among the vilest and most perverted cities within traveling distance of the Sea of Galilee. Why would Jesus choose this place and name the gates of hell as a reference point for the construction of His church?

Perhaps when Jesus said "upon this rock," He was referring to something they were seeing with their own eyes. In other words, the church was to be built in the most degenerate and distorted places—the places that had regressed into inhumanity in the most devolved of ways and had crafted the most outlandish assumptions about who God is and how to connect with Him.

Maybe the church is to be built in those places so that the distorted assumptions about God might be righted and none may enter the gates of hell. These places are exactly where the "church" of Jesus' time wouldn't even go. They had, in many ways, crafted assumptions of their own about God through their traditions and rituals—assumptions that eventually made them accomplices in killing God on a cross.

Perhaps with this question, Jesus was once again revealing how we've gotten things almost backward from the way they were intended to be.

The thing is, all of these explanations are irrelevant without an answer to the original question: "Who do you say that I am?" Unless we push through to what is true about Jesus, and what is true about us, we will never see things rightly.

Jesus' question is an invitation to cut through every false assumption in our lives and declare a truth that roots our souls in a place that cannot be shaken. Knowing who Jesus is, and living from that place, anchors us in true humanity— which is how Jesus lived. We have no examples in the Gospels of Jesus leaping to false conclusions or assumptions. Jesus always looked beyond what was being presented to Him to discern what was really going on.

It's not too difficult to find our own versions of Caesarea Philippi in the modern world. The gates of hell aren't hard to spot, but can the church that Jesus spoke of be spotted there? Is the Kingdom going there? Is life breaking out and redemption flourishing? Not unless God's people are there as His hands and feet—hands and feet that have moved behind the façade of assumption, false reality, and fear in order to actually engage.

But what does actually engaging look like?

I've traveled hundreds of thousands of miles of roadway, and rarely do I travel a great distance without passing a billboard that reads, "We bare all," with the promise of unspoken tantalizing pleasures. But I wonder—illicit encounters aside—what might it be like if this were the trademark of the church Jesus foretold? What if "We bare all" were our motto, evidenced by our assumption-free lives of identity and purpose? What if there were nothing to hide because (to quote Paul from 1 Corinthians) we "bear all things"? It requires great inner strength to *bare* ourselves in new and vulnerable ways that awaken our utter dependence on God for life and identity. As Paul pointed out, though, *bearing* this burden is part of the Christian life. What if we could simply live true like Jesus? In this we can, and in fact must, pay one thing: attention.

Our humanity is not something that is happening to us. We are happening to it. Every choice is one of sanctification or regression. Every decision is one of redemption or transgression. We're either creating the world Jesus envisioned—a world where we live out of a true place, where we have nothing to hide—or swinging the sledgehammer of assumption and isolation to destroy it. Everything we do is building the church or tearing it down, and every allegiance is either to the Kingdom of Heaven or to that of darkness. And make no mistake: We get to choose—and we do. We can use our creative energy to manufacture false realities, or we can use that same energy to confront what is false in this world. The battle begins inside our own souls.

As we talked about at the beginning of this book, humanity made a trade in the Garden of Eden. We had the truth, and we traded it for knowledge—and we've been trying to use our knowledge to find truth ever since. But truth cannot be found without God. We cannot be true or truly human without God. Jesus showed us what it looks like to be a true and assumption-free human being with nothing false at all lurking in the shadows.

Jesus was the human God. I know that seems jolting, and if it's not jolting, we need to think harder about what it actually means. Because this is at the very heart of the gospel. None of it holds together unless Jesus was fully God and fully human. And as we've explored before, this human God spent His earthly life showing us how He intended for us to live—what our normal is supposed to look like. Jesus wasn't inviting us into a life that we cannot possibly have. He wasn't offering the best Christmas present ever and then pulling it back at the last second as a dark, cosmic prank. He invites us into the life of Christ: a life utterly dependent and fully intertwined with God, where anything is possible—a life that is true and normal.

The Scriptures tell us that we are His body,[2] His church,[3] and His Kingdom is within us.[4] Either it's true or it isn't. We aren't "sort of" any of these things.

48

If we're going to be Christ-like, then we must be true all the way to our core identity. What is false should be seen for the poison it is to our souls.

This church that Jesus spoke of is an expressly human thing. And it is in the process of happening right now.

We must learn to actively engage ourselves and become aware of what God is doing—as if we'd just had a bucket of ice water thrown in our faces. We must pay attention as if our lives depend on it. God is on the move reclaiming our species. Are we being pulled forward into a true and divine nature[5] or degenerating into a false and iniquitous one, full of fabricated reality and assumption? We get to choose. Emancipation is a gift—and a choice. We've been living as animals for too long, all the while sensing the deep and ancient longing for redemption and shalom—the wholeness of a human life intertwined with the divine nature of the Spirit of God within us. We long for a life that is true in a world that is true.

But what would this even look like?

Ah, but it's here, available, and now!

From mountaintops to lands at the bottom of the earth, I have seen God on the move. Even in places I would have never expected Him. Life is defying death everywhere. Look about you and see what is true.

The beauty of this planet has no known rival but Heaven itself. There is no match for the artistry of God, and there is no ignoring His presence and Kingdom in and among us. Wake up and see what is true.

Look in the mirror and confront what is false in you. Beneath it all you will find what is true—you will find the Spirit of Christ within. Open your eyes and see.

Everything we do of art and beauty is nothing but the hope of capturing one fleeting moment—a ghost of the glory that has created and is sustaining the world. We are made of this and for this as image bearers of God. This is a picture of our true humanity. It is a picture of what is true.

Together we spin on this big beautiful rock we call home. And upon this rock Jesus will build His church, and the gates of hell will not prevail against it.

You are invited into this. Why continue to doubt it? Why not fully engage with heart, mind, and will? Why not become Christ-like? Why not become fully human? Why not become true?

What about you? Who do you say that Jesus is?

06.

Keratoconus

On miracles

Miracles in fact are a retelling in small letters of the
very same story which is written across the whole
world in letters too large for some of us to see.

C. S. LEWIS

THE ENTRANCE RAMP onto westbound I-84 seemed like a causeway into hell. Just hours earlier, I'd been in a sandstorm to the north, and now my eyes were grit-laden and screaming.

Let me explain. I have a rare eye condition known as keratoconus. Basically my corneas protrude in the center, creating a subtle bulge or cone. The complicated part is how my brain interprets light. When light hits a normal spherical cornea, it is uniformly transmitted to the retina and deciphered by the brain. This is how we see.

In my case, light passes through my corneas in a spray of light and color. If you smear a thin layer of Vaseline on the

lenses of your glasses, you'll have a reasonable approxima-
tion. I feel like I'm able to see a dozen of the same images all
smeared together at the same time—awesome for Christmas
lights, but terrible other than that.

To correct the problem, I have to wear rigid contact lenses
that vault over the coned area and fill with tears. This creates
a normal sphere for my brain to interpret. But when something like sand gets into my eyes and begins to grate at the
edges of the contacts and scrape away at my eyelids . . . well,
you can imagine what a big deal it is.

The sun was a blister of orange sitting directly at the end
of the highway with nary a tree, rock, or butte to give me
a moment of amnesty. I felt as though I were driving into a
migraine.

To cope, I put on two pairs of sunglasses. The pair closest
to my eyes was just a step below welding glasses. I could barely
see the road. (Thankfully I had it all to myself.)

"I can't see!" I shouted at the sun, which of course remained indifferent.

After thirty minutes, the hateful red fireball began to slip
below the horizon. As I took the glasses off, the sky exploded
in crimson, peach, lavender, and indigo. The desert stars were
as pinpricks into the glory of God. I was still in a lot of
pain, but it was mixed with an equal amount of wonder.
My eyes were scratched, scorched, and brutally irritated, but
they were beholding majesty. What had been a cause of suffering only moments before had turned into the ever-present
miraculous all around me.

I'm obviously not the only person in the world who has had to deal with vision problems. Long ago there was a man who described quite remarkably the way my eyes see. He was standing before Jesus, discussing his own vision issues.

"I see men as trees, walking," he told Jesus.[1]

This was, ironically, an improvement. The man had been completely blind moments before.

They were in Bethsaida—a small fishing village near the Sea of Galilee. The remnants of this same village endure today. It's one of my favorite places in Israel. Not many go there, but its pastoral setting among the lush hills feels haunted with the presence of Jesus.

This man had been led to Jesus, who had subsequently taken him outside the city and spit in his eyes. A little weird, I admit. But nonetheless, while only moments before the man had lived in darkness, he now saw people like trees, walking. Jesus touched his eyes again, and suddenly the man could see perfectly. Jesus told the man to go home but warned him not to go back into the village—presumably so that no one would know.

Why did He try to keep the miracle a secret? If any of us could perform miracles, wouldn't we want people to know?

Downplaying miracles was a common thing with Jesus. He was a part of thirty-seven miracles, according to the Gospels. And that's just what we know about from the Scriptures. The apostle John said there were many more.[2] In twenty-one of these instances, Jesus told people to keep quiet about it, did it in a private way, or was a seemingly reluctant or coincidental participant. Needing a crowd to witness was never Jesus' style. He didn't grandstand. It's hard to imagine, but on a number of occasions He had to defend Himself for healing someone because it was a holy day.

Maybe showing the world what He could do wasn't the point. Maybe it was all about the person in front of Him.

Prior to the miraculous taking place, Jesus often asked miraclees if they believed He could do it. Sometimes, He asked them to articulate what they wanted Him to do for them. And many times after miracles, He told the miraclees to go in peace—their faith had made them whole.

This interaction—this give and take—is a part of most of Jesus' miracles. It's as if the miracle wouldn't have happened without the hope, agreement, faith, and openness of the partaker. It wasn't just Jesus doing something to a person; it was Jesus awakening something deep within that person that collaborated with the power of God.

Take the bleeding woman, for example.[3] Jesus was on His way to deal with an entirely different matter when this encounter happened. The woman had been bleeding for twelve years. One can only imagine the burden and humiliation in her life.

As a man, I cannot relate. However, I do have a wife and a daughter, and I can't imagine that a twelve-year period would have been easy for this woman or anyone else in her life. And it wasn't as if she hadn't tried to get well. She'd spent everything she could earn to pay her medical bills, but no one could help her.

The rumors of a rabbi who could heal sparked something buried deep within this woman: hope. She knew that if she ever got the chance, she would find Him. But she couldn't simply approach Him directly. There were a number of formidable obstacles: She was a woman in a patriarchal culture; the crowds were overwhelming; and, most delicately, she was unclean. According to Mosaic law, her bleeding meant that she was perpetually unclean. If she touched a rabbi and made him unclean on purpose, she would at best be publicly humiliated.

She followed the crowd for the same reason people buy lottery tickets: A miracle *could* happen. She began an internal conversation: *If I could get close enough just to brush His clothes, I think I would be healed.*

And when the opportunity came, she reached out before she could think.

It worked. She could feel the change immediately. But she was also busted.

Jesus stopped and began looking around. "Who touched me?" He asked.

The disciples laughed.

"Everyone is touching You, Jesus," they said.

Her plan had been solid. The disciples had validated this—everyone was touching Him. She just hadn't accounted for the fact that the Healer might know what had happened. She had no choice but to come clean.

As she stepped toward Jesus, her story spilled from her lips. Jesus' eyes drew her in like a magnet. His kind grin widened. "Your suffering is over, daughter," He said. "Go in peace. Your faith has made you whole."

This story is beautiful, and again we see the collaboration that Jesus invites a person into. Each miracle was as if He were awakening in them something alive and true and already present.

Another blind man, this one named Bartimaeus, is also a good example of this awakening. Bartimaeus lived near the Dead Sea in one of the world's most ancient cities: Jericho.[4]

Jesus had a lot on His mind on this trip through the city. He was on His way to Jerusalem, where the icy hand of death awaited Him.

Bartimaeus begged for charity to survive. He knew about Jesus' reputation, and when Jesus passed by, he was desperate enough to scream in hope that Jesus might actually hear him.

The crowd mobbing Jesus did everything they could to shut down Bartimaeus, but he just yelled louder. Against the odds, Jesus stopped and asked for the man to be brought to Him.

"What do you want Me to do for you?" Jesus asked.

"I want to see," Bartimaeus stammered in reply.

Again we see Jesus invite someone to collaborate in the process—and the man got what he asked for. His eyes were opened, and Jesus told him that it was his faith that had healed him.

Was Jesus being overly modest in not taking the credit

due Him in these miracles? Or was He speaking the simple truth?

Jesus talked about miracles as if they're supposed to be normal: "I tell you the truth, anyone who believes in me will do the same works I have done, and even greater works, because I am going to be with the Father."[5]

Apparently the miraculous is supposed to be a normal part of the life of a normal human being—a person utterly dependent on and consciously intertwined with the Spirit of God. Perhaps collaborating in the miraculous should be a part of our everyday lives.

Maybe we're missing things all around us that we can't explain because they are ubiquitous. Like the introspective longing we feel at the song of crickets on a summer evening. Or the call of the angry ocean that is at once terrifying and awe inspiring. None of these things can really be explained or even defined, but things like this happen to us all the time.

Maybe we're missing the miraculous occurring everywhere. And maybe if we became aware, we would understand how much we are collaborating in it—or working against it.

This evening on my porch I watched the sunset. Delicate wisps of charcoal and granite around the edges gave outline and shadow to the explosion of cobalt, lavender, and blood orange bursting across the sky. And it wasn't as if earthbound nature weren't involved. The hills were an inferno, and the leaves were shimmering as if in worship. Every color harmonized with the others, and I found this remarkable. In nature, nothing contrasts harshly. Hints of Eden—the way things were meant to be.

The entire sunset was spellbinding, enthralling, and even miraculous. And that was only tonight. Miracles are everywhere if only we pay attention.

Jesus' first recorded miracle was of changing water into wine. It made for a great wedding celebration, but was it really just a one-off? After all, water is still being turned into wine. Maybe we're just not paying attention to the constellation of miracles that collaborate to make it happen: Water miraculously falls from the sky, saturating the earth. The earth absorbs the water and enriches and miraculously nourishes the vine. The vine feeds the grape as the sun collaborates by heating the earth, which not only supports life on this planet but also nourishes both vine and grape in miraculous ways. And the miracles continue at the cellular level, day and night, in the soil, the vine, and the grape. All of these miracles conspire to create a beautiful, robust grape that is then harvested and treated—humans continue to collaborate in the miracle through harvesting, fermenting, blending. At the end of it all, wine is bottled and savored. Water has become wine.

When we get down to it, it's hard to find something that *isn't* miraculous. It's a miracle that we're even here, no matter how you look at it. We're living in the middle of a miracle at this very moment. And to simply become aware of it may be as easy as truly realizing our utter dependence on God for absolutely everything—and His good pleasure in giving it to us moment by miraculous moment. This is Jesus' invitation: to fully exhale and fall face-first into what our normal should be like—the human and the divine conspiring to make us who we are and collaborating in the miraculous all around us.

07

Neighbors

On Samaritans in pickup trucks

Not everyone who has helped or is helping
you wanted or wants to help you.
MOKOKOMA MOKHONOANA

OUTSIDE OF THE JOSHUA TREE Wilderness in California, just past the junction where Highways 62 and 177 meet, the road begins to descend into a deep desert valley, cutting a razor-straight line all the way to the horizon. It's quite staggering in its ruggedness. In the little patch where the roads meet, you'll find a stop sign. Ten miles west is where I got stranded. I had simply pulled off to the side of the road to take a picture, but the shoulder was made of soft sand, and my truck sank into it like butter. It was 112 degrees Fahrenheit. The nearest town was more than thirty miles away.

I rocked the truck back and forth a little, but it was no

use. It was buried to the axles, and as I took the proverbial deep breath, I told myself not to panic. I had gallons of water. I would live through this.

I tried to call for help, but my phone offered me a useless "no service" indicator. Cold-hearted little voices in the back of my mind started saying naughty things about rattlesnakes and scorpions.

Seeing no other alternative, I began to dig with my hands, only to realize that baking sand caused blisters. I should also mention that in the first hour only one car had passed on the other side of the road.

It was about a half-hour later when an open-topped Jeep flew by. I looked up and saw the red glow of brake lights, and a minute later the Jeep circled back to me. I didn't even pretend I wasn't in trouble when the driver asked if I needed a lift. I climbed aboard with a liter and a half of water in each hand.

"Rough place to get stuck," the good Samaritan yelled over the whip of the wind as he started driving again. His son sat in the back, sizing me up.

"Yeah," I said. "Sure is."

"You'll never dig out of that," he said.

"I was coming to that conclusion," I said.

"Tow truck's gonna be hard to find out here. Nearest town's thirty miles, and it's nothin'."

"Hmm," I said.

It went on like that for a while. We talked into the twilight as the temperature dropped below 100. They had been at Lake Havasu to Jet Ski, which apparently is a big deal to the desert folk. He'd migrated to the desert to escape the city and make a life for his family. We made small talk until we came to the edge of town, where he pulled in front of a run-down honky-tonk of a bar and told me there was a phone and that if there was a tow truck within a hundred miles, the people inside would know how to locate it.

I waved as the people who seemed to be my only friends drove off in a cloud of dust.

Under normal circumstances, I would have probably never given this man the time of day. And to be honest, if the shoe had been on the other foot, I would have probably driven right past myself out of fear of an ambush or some other deep desert folly. This man had been kindhearted enough to be neighborly.

In the Gospel of Luke, Jesus was asked an interesting question: "Who is my neighbor?"[1]

It was actually a follow-up to a question an expert in religious law had been asking. His leading question had been more of a softball: "What must I do to inherit eternal life?"[2]

Jesus' response was fascinatingly Jewish: "You're an expert. What does the Scripture say? How do you read it?"[3] The invitation to ask questions of the Scriptures and wrestle with the ideas they bring up has always been a part of the Jewish tradition and culture. The Jews were the children of Israel—*Israel* meaning "One who wrestles with God."[4]

This contrasts rather dramatically with the more modern approach of attempting to squash questions and doubt like unwanted roaches, as if God were too nervous and uptight to deal with all of that.

Rather than being lofty, Jesus invited discourse even though he was being tested. He was willing to wrestle with the ideas. It's beautiful, really—God inviting a man to discuss the way he understands the Scripture.

The answer given was the traditional one—to keep the great commandments.

"'You must love the LORD your God with all your heart, all your soul, all your strength, and all your mind.' And, 'Love your neighbor as yourself,'" he said.[5] To which Jesus replied, "Good answer. If you do this you will live."[6]

But the man wasn't done with questions. "Who is my neighbor?" he asked.[7]

———

In the desert, I had found the kind of neighbor Jesus talked about. And I probably wouldn't have been that kind of neighbor myself, had I been in his shoes. I was deeply grateful for the kindness that had rescued me.

I took another deep breath and did a slow, full turn in the parking lot. To the east was the dark, empty road that led to my truck. To the west was a sliver of light in the distant sky— just enough to backlight the mountains and make them ominous. I turned to face the mostly broken neon sign over a rusted awning. The neon was flickering, of course. There was an old gas station sign swinging wearily in the breeze. Honestly, it felt as if I had walked into a cliché. Stepping to the pay phone, I wondered whom I might call. I was completely on my own, after all. I was the only person I knew for hundreds of miles.

Resigned, I stepped into the bar, and immediately all four patrons whirled around to stare at me. On the far right of the bar was a huge, muscle-bound man with dreadlocks and a crimson sleeveless T-shirt. Next to him was a man in his sixties with stringy, shoulder-length gray hair and a long gray beard. The bartender looked like his brother. The man on the left side of the bar was a younger, shorter, stocky man who looked like he had something to prove.

I got the distinct impression that I was not welcome. I wondered if I should back out slowly or risk never being found again.

"Hey guys," I said.

No response.

"You wouldn't happen to know where there might be a tow truck around here, would you?" I felt like an eight-year-old.

Nothing.

I followed the muscleman's eyes as he glanced across the bar. The stocky guy stood and took a step toward me.

"It'll cost you fifty bucks for me to even fire it up," he said.

"That will be fine," I said.

His eyebrows rose a little.

"You got cash?" he asked.

This was a precarious question.

"I think I might have fifty in cash. I don't really carry much cash. You don't take credit cards, do you?"

He just stared. I assumed it was a no.

I reached in my pocket and cobbled together the fee. I even scraped out a few single dollar bills to make the fifty, trying to show them it was all I had and that stealing my pants and throwing me out on the road wasn't worth the trouble. For added effect I said, "Man, I wish you did take cards because I'd buy you guys a round just for helping me out like this."

Bingo. Even though it wouldn't be happening, somehow the thought of using my money to buy their beer helped warm the atmosphere . . . slightly.

The stocky guy took the cash and headed out the door, telling me he'd be back with the tow truck. I was left alone with two guys, who looked like prophets, and their bodyguard. No one was saying a word. Six eyes were trained on me like rifles. It was dreadfully uncomfortable. What did I have in common with these people? How could I possibly begin a conversation? How could we be neighborly with suspicion hanging in the air like a cloud?

"Whatcha got in the backpack?" one of the prophets asked. And I realized that they were on high alert about me as much as I was about them.

"I've got some water and my cameras," I said.

"You a photographer?"

"Sort of," I said. "I've been shooting in the desert for a couple of days."

A laugh. Then another. Then they were all laughing.

"It's beautiful out there," I said.

They nodded while snickering at me.

Were we becoming friendly? I didn't know, but the tension had become more manageable. I had made assumptions about these people based on the surreal circumstances I was in. They had made assumptions about me because I was most certainly not one of their tribe.

———

To answer the question "Who is my neighbor?" Jesus told a story.

A man was on his way from Jerusalem to Jericho. The route was an ancient pathway that everyone knew about— from Jerusalem at 2,500 feet above sea level, down eighteen miles to Jericho at just more than eight hundred feet below sea level. The open and fertile region surrounding the hill country of Jerusalem dropped down into a stark and desolate wasteland very similar to the one I had been stranded in. It was a dangerous road, notorious for desert bandits. Much earlier, King David referred to it as "the valley of the shadow of death," in a song that became Psalm 23.

The man in Jesus' story fell into the hands of bandits, who beat him senseless, stole everything he had, stripped him naked, and left him for dead on the side of the road.

A priest came along but when he saw the man, he moved to the other side of the path and kept moving. There could have been any number of reasons for this. He could have thought the man was dead. He could have been obeying the letter of the law—touching a corpse would have made him unclean. He could have thought the man was a decoy and bandits were waiting in ambush. All we know is that he kept moving. The scene is unsettling because this would probably have been me. I would have driven past myself on the side of the desert road. I would have kept moving by this man out of fear of what could happen to me.

Next a temple assistant happened by. Perhaps he couldn't determine whether the man was alive or dead, but he also kept moving along.

Then a Samaritan man came along, and things changed, just as things changed for me that night in the lonely Mojave.

———

The bar door flung open and the stocky guy came back in. He grabbed his beer off the bar and drained the entire can, belched loudly, and beckoned me out to the truck.

Following him I noticed that the "tow truck" was actually an old Ford pickup—probably a late '70s model. My new companion checked the gas gauge before jumping out of the cab and rummaging in the truck bed, which was filled with all sorts of construction tools.

"We better make sure there's some extra gas back here." He burped. "Nobody goes out there in the dark much."

"Ah," I said, looking around for a gas can. I spotted an old five-gallon water container filled to about the two-gallon mark and pointed it out.

"That ain't gas," he said.

"Ah," I replied, trying to reason out the need to collect urine in the wide-open desert, where options for disposal are nearly limitless.

After a couple of minutes, I began to realize that my new friend was drunk. This gave me pause. I wondered if he would let me drive. I didn't think so. I scanned my options. There weren't any. I climbed into the passenger's seat, reasoning that there would be no oncoming traffic and the greatest danger was him driving off the road. I positioned myself so I could grab the wheel if he passed out and decided I would have to steel myself for something I have very little skill for: small talk. As we drove into the blackness, I breathed an earnest plea to Jesus.

My companion turned out to be more colorful than I'd imagined. The first fifteen minutes I didn't have to say much, but I did learn a great deal about the desert female population. This was followed by an illuminating discourse on his personal experiences in that area. I figured that as long as he kept talking about the ladies, he would probably stay awake.

Conversation meandered to his work in construction and masonry. He mostly laid stone, he told me. Then he went back to talking about women, so I attempted to move the conversation to something that particularly interested me.

"How do you think we'll get my truck out of the sand?" I asked.

"We'll rip it out one way or another," he told me—a troubling statement, as my truck was a rental.

Then he nodded off, and I stopped worrying about the rental truck.

"So!" I yelled, and he lifted his head back up. "How many rattlesnakes have you seen out here?"

I then received a very detailed and colorful oration on rattlesnakes that fundamentally breaks down to this: If you back a rattlesnake into a corner, it will try to strike you. Rattlesnakes prefer to be left alone, and if you back away from them slowly, they will go back to whatever they were doing. How you handle your fear will determine your fate.

When I think about Jesus' story of the beaten man on the side of the road, fear seems to be the rattlesnake in the bushes that strikes out. It overrides our compassion. It's not that on any given day we've purposely set out to be aloof or uncaring. Our hearts reach out when we see misfortune in the world. Isn't it the concern about getting entangled in the unknown that often keeps us moving by? This is why I would have probably driven past myself on the side of the road: the fear of what I might be getting myself into. I wouldn't have loved my neighbor as myself; I would have just protected myself.

The fear of involvement also kept two men in Jesus' story from helping a dying man on the side of the road. Listeners—then as now—naturally look at them unfavorably for their lack of compassion. But aren't we still doing this all the time in subtle ways?

We've been segregating ourselves into camps of thought and conviction for thousands of years because of the fear of what one person or ideology can do to another. And the fear is legitimate. In our broken humanity, people have always managed to find ways to be brutal to one another. Is there a balance? Can we love our neighbor while protecting ourselves from them? Can we truly love anyone without becoming vulnerable in some way?

Everyone is capable of hurting someone else. And everyone is capable of showing astounding benevolence. In some ways it boils down to whether we're paying attention to what is happening around us—and how we manage our fear when we face the rattlesnake.

Nevertheless, these human fears seem starkly contrasted to the commandment, "Love your neighbor as yourself."

Jesus fearlessly brushed shoulders with the zealot, the elite, and everyone in between. He was comfortable in His own skin and comfortable entering into the stories of whomever He was among. This contrasts with our own attempts at self-preservation and confronts us in disruptive ways. Whereas we often don't look at someone long enough to see anything but a rattlesnake, Jesus saw everyone as a person with a story to tell. Perhaps if we observed this commandment fully, we would find our hearts unshackled, our fear and isolation diluted and dissolved, and our humanity becoming just a little more like Jesus.

In a desert that was completely indifferent to me, I met compassion and rescue. In the rescue I found myself riding shotgun in the dark with a fellow human being with whom

I had little in common. But there we were, collaborating on a mission that neither one of us would have imagined only hours before. I was treated as a neighbor by people I would have driven by or ignored. I was shown mercy in ways that I would likely not have offered. And as my neighbor chained the trucks together, I felt a wave of gratitude—this would all be over soon.

Once the vehicles were fastened, it was time for the extraction. My friend sat in my truck and I sat in his while we tried to rock things free. This was unsuccessful. He then decided that we should pull the truck out in reverse. This was also unsuccessful. After about a half hour of failed attempts, I began to see glimpses of my friend's spirituality. He kicked sand and smacked metal and called out to Christ and Mary and the angels. In a loud voice he asked God to cast down vengeful judgment against the trucks. This went on for several minutes—then he went completely silent. For thirty seconds only the stillness of the desert and the whisper of a breeze could be heard. I wasn't sure if he was listening for a response from the Lord or if he'd passed out.

Then he spoke in a measured monotone: "You get in your truck and I'll pull in mine. We're getting this [redacted] [redacted] piece of [redacted] out of this [redacted] [redacted] sand right this [redacted] [redacted] minute," he told me, and although he articulated it differently from how I might have chosen, we were fundamentally in agreement. I obediently climbed into my truck.

He went off like a madman. We were pulling and yanking

and getting a little running start—and we'd managed to move my truck about a foot. We looked it over for a minute, and he jumped back in his truck. I did the same. And then I heard a distinct snap followed by a hiss.

The older truck had smoke coming from beneath the hood and appeared to be urinating on the road. My friend was not happy. He hurled insults and invoked the Lord's wrath against the truck again.

I began to realize something quite unnerving—now we were both stuck in the desert with no way out. I'd made all the small talk I could. He was drunk and unpredictable, and we were facing the prospect of a cozy evening together. I chuckled in disbelief. I had indeed gained some knowledge of and a little respect for my new friend, but not enough to spend the night together.

During the whole ordeal I had been arrogantly looking down my nose at this man as a drunken desert rat, and he had been looking at me as a clueless city boy. But under the desert stars we were simply two people trying to get free. And to be honest, my friend had left a comfortable evening with his friends to help me. It was more than the fifty bucks between us now. We had struggled together, and his resolve to see it through was striking.

———

The hero in Jesus' story was also an unlikely one. It's complicated and nuanced (as life can sometimes be), but Samaritans were typically outcasts who were only grudgingly tolerated.

They didn't believe the same way, they were thought to be untrustworthy, they practiced corrupted customs, and as a result they were marginalized. For Jesus to make a Samaritan the hero of the story was as unsettling as He intended it to be.

Think of the person you most dislike or the people group that most terrifies you, and then imagine them saving your life. And not just saving your life but also paying your medical bills and checking on you to make sure you were restored to health. This is what Jesus was inviting His listeners to contemplate as they considered loving their neighbors as themselves. Jesus invited them to consider their own bias and prejudice. He was masterfully moving behind culture's venomous snakebite of assumption and fear and calling out to what was human. To love your neighbor as yourself is an expressly human thing.

I admit this isn't easy. Jesus was essentially saying that when by chance we encounter fellow human beings with an obvious need, they are our neighbors regardless of how different they are from us, and we are to love them. We are to move behind our own stereotypes, fears, and prejudices and see another human being created in the image of God. Even more, we're to look for the face of Jesus in them.[8]

In the desert I began to fear that my truck would not be freed before the sunrise. I began to contemplate whether my friend and I would have to spend the night out there. But my assumptions of this man were also being reshaped. He had incredible grit and determination regardless of his level of intoxication. I could see the frustration and loneliness in him. He had escaped my stereotype and had become a man with a story of his own. And this is how I think we each break through and see people as our neighbors.

I pondered upon this until he asked me for the keys. He walked the ten yards to my truck, and then everything turned into a war zone. I had to take cover behind his truck. Back and forth and back and forth he rocked the truck with debris flying like shrapnel everywhere, but I'll be darned if he wasn't making progress. A minute later my truck was out of the sand with four wheels safely on asphalt.

He leaped out of my truck and yelled, "You're mine! You're mine, you [redacted] [redacted]! You think you can take me, you [redacted] little [redacted]?" Then he was done.

"You're unstuck," he mentioned, walking over to me.

"I'm pretty excited about that," I said.

"Dude's not going to be too happy, though. We ruined his truck," he said.

"What can I do to help?" I asked.

"Forget it." He laughed. "He'll have to come out here and get it tomorrow."

We pushed the old warrior to the side of the road near where I'd been pinned in. I then made a beeline toward my driver's seat.

"Let me give you a ride back," I said.

He climbed into the passenger seat, and we rolled away. I'd assumed he would have more to share with me about stonemasonry and desert heat, beer, and ladies, but he fell fast asleep and that was probably for the best. Forty minutes later I was pulling into the roadhouse and waking my disoriented friend.

The whole episode had been so surreal that I had to go back inside just to get one last look. I grabbed my camera, and when I walked through the door it was as if I had crossed a threshold of acceptance and been furnished with friendship and neighborly goodwill. I was taking pictures of everyone and telling them that I'd send prints. They were telling me that I knew where to get stuck next time I was out there.

———

Humanity and divinity have to collaborate in order for us to love our neighbors as ourselves. We're not capable of navigating this any other way. When Jesus concluded His story, He asked which of the men traveling on the dangerous road proved to be the neighbor.

"The one who showed mercy," replied the religious leader.

"Go and do the same," Jesus concluded. And that is what sticks with me most about this story—go and do the same. Go and show mercy when the chance is given.

To love our neighbor as ourselves is not something we can conjure up. We can love those who are familiar to us, but to look beyond a stereotype or assumption and see a human being in need requires vulnerability, courage, awareness, and faith. These are not things we can master without collaborating with God. And perhaps this is the point.

The two great commandments are intertwined in this story, and one does not go without the other. We cannot love our neighbors as ourselves if we do not love God with all that we are. We were never created to do this without God involved intimately. These commandments cannot be obeyed without the human and divine intertwined and in collaboration.

Commingled and in collaboration with Jesus, we can allow the love of God to pulse with every beat of our hearts. And the force and weight of our lives can be an expression of God's love for the world.

It's idealistic to think of a world like this, I know. Maybe it's impossible. But this is the posture of the Kingdom of Heaven Jesus constantly spoke of—a Kingdom we are a part of and are supposed to be representing right now.

May we love the Lord our God with all our heart, mind, and strength. And may we love our neighbors as ourselves, for this is what it looks like to be a true human—a person who is like Christ.

08

Open It Up

On rolling stones and resurrections

A bridge of silver wings stretches
from the dead ashes of an unforgiving nightmare
to the jeweled vision of a life started anew.

ABERJHANI,
"THE RIVER OF WINGED DREAMS"

THE FIRST SHADES OF AUTUMN peeked through the trees while thin ribbons of cloud collected the sun's warmth. It was a gorgeous day that would soon dip into unexpected melancholy. I had traveled to South Carolina for a speaking event, and afterward I was given the opportunity to visit the site of one of the largest Christian ministries the world has ever known. When I was a child, the place drew millions of visitors every year. Thousands of acres of beauty surrounded a world-class broadcast studio that beamed daily messages of hope all around the world. But it's all gone now. Only a few structures remain, and those are being slowly reclaimed by nature or repurposed for other use. The beautifully groomed acreage has been broken into subdivisions for middle-class Americans who are probably unaware of the history beneath their manicured lawns.

Walking the remaining grounds, I felt myself sinking. Spaces once so full of life were just a shell of what they used to be. As I stared into the empty hull of a high-rise hotel, I felt my heart pulled toward places in Israel like Capernaum and Bethsaida, ruins of settlements and villages where Jesus ate, slept, and breathed. Shells. Reminders. Remnants of a thing that once was.

It was a very discouraging couple of hours. I thought about the millions of dollars that went into the creation of the grounds and all of the broadcasting of the gospel of Jesus Christ. It all ended up in ruins.

So who am I to think I'll ever make a dent? I wondered. *Most of those who heard Jesus speak didn't believe Him, so who am I to do any better? If Jesus was God wrapped in humanity, then apparently God wasn't compelling enough even to keep His own hometown alive. Who am I to think I'm going to have any better chance with anything I ever do?*

As lost as I was in my own head, I began to come to terms with the fact that Jesus' message wasn't really about geography or ornate buildings. Every building becomes a ruin sooner or later. Jesus came to rebuild ruins of a different kind.

Jesus came to bring life back to the ruins of the soul and reveal how humanity was intended to be—but most people didn't fully embrace or even understand Him. They flocked to Him because He could heal the sick, but they saw Him simply as an anomaly or magic man. I am no different. I have followed Jesus because the stories of His miraculous deeds offer proof that He was something out of the ordinary. But His words and posture reveal that His objective was far more profound than the flashy miracles we are drawn to. We've been hung up on the magic, but He was calling out our true humanity, leading us back toward our identity, and rebuilding the ruins of our souls the whole time.

In this work of rebuilding souls, Jesus wasn't modeling something we're simply to aspire to. He was showing us who we are: restored humans, meant to live out of our normal human state. If we were to embrace this truth, the world would be overrun with wholeness and the ever-present Spirit of God among us. Can you even imagine that?

But as I wrestled with this idea, I was forced to enter my own doubt and disillusionment. Is being Christ-like an ambition, or is it a reality in my own heart? Where am I still living out of a subhuman state? What places inside me are in ruins in need of restoration? Has Jesus been able to reclaim all of the ruined places within my humanity and rebuild wholeness?

———

In John's Gospel we find the story of the resurrection of Lazarus.[1] As happens often when we approach Scripture, it's easy to focus on the miracle and miss the underlying humanity, ruin, and loss contained in the story. Jesus entered into these situations seeing the whole. He knew that the exterior ruins of the world were simply evidence of what was ruined in the soul. We see these things most clearly in the shortest verse in the Bible, two very human words that describe a very human act but are loaded with complexity and richness:

"Jesus wept."[2]

The death of Lazarus, and everything that follows, is filled with deep humanity—and with divine possibility lurking around the edges, as is the case in all of life.

The drama began to unfold when Jesus walked into the little suburb of Jerusalem known as Bethany. When Lazarus's sister Martha heard the commotion, she immediately ran out to meet Jesus, in tears. Almost accusingly, she told Him that if He had just been there, none of this would have happened—Lazarus wouldn't have died.

This is such a profoundly human response to God. I've said those words so many times. Haven't you?

"Jesus, if You had just been here, my marriage wouldn't be in ruins."

"Jesus, if You had just been here, my job wouldn't be in ruins."

"Jesus, if You had just been here, my health wouldn't be in ruins."

Jesus, if You had just been here.

In an attempt to comfort Martha, Jesus offered hope that Lazarus would rise again—and she totally dismissed the idea. She couldn't grasp that Jesus might be referring to something immediate and not in a distant and mysterious eternity. Martha told Jesus that she *knew* Lazarus would rise again *someday*, but the implication was that for now, there was no going back. He was dead. He'd been buried. It was over.[3]

That's when Jesus told her that He was the resurrection and the life—and that what had died would live even though it died.

I know. It gets a little complicated, but stay with me.

Martha apparently nodded affirmatively and filed it away as another Jesus-ism, because she moved right past the resurrection talk and told Him that she did believe He was God's Son.

Minutes later Martha's sister, Mary, met Jesus on the path. She was so distraught and grief stricken that she fell to the ground, blocking Jesus' path. Her message was the same: "If You had just been here . . ."

The little village of Bethany had collected together to grieve the loss of their beloved Lazarus, and Jesus was overcome with human emotion at the sight. He looked upon the sadness and loss and began to weep salty human tears along with them. He was certainly grieving, but His tears went deeper than grief.

When loss and ruin come—and they do for us all—it's normal to grieve. It's also normal to be angry and troubled, as the Scriptures indicate Jesus was.[4] These are normal human responses to loss, but Jesus wasn't simply grieving—He was frustrated. He was looking beyond the loss of a friend and seeing the bigger picture. He knew that more was going on than anyone else saw. The grief and loss touched the physical, emotional, and spiritual. The ruin of death and loss of

Lazarus's presence spoke also, and more truly, of the ruin of the soul and longing for restoration. Jesus was grieving the fact that His friends were ruined by a finality that was not final.

Jesus asked to be immediately taken to the tomb where they had laid the body. He followed the dusty path behind the mourning sisters and then did something unthinkable.

"Open it up," He told them.

They turned to each other in astonishment. Jesus repeated Himself, telling them to roll away the stone that was covering the burial cave.

"Jesus," they said, "he's been in there for four days. He's dead. His body is decaying. He stinks."

Jesus was remarkably resolute. The mourners probably thought this was a demonstration of His love for the dead man: Clearly Jesus wanted to pay His respects regardless of the odor. But something rose up within Jesus that transcended their collective grief.

"Didn't I tell you that if you would just believe me, you would see the glory of God in all of this?" He asked.[5] In other words, the devastating loss and ruins of their lives were not the final word.

Tentatively a few of the men acquiesced. With covered faces they shoved the entry stone aside, expecting the fresh, wet, pungent stench of human decay to spill from the cave.

The villagers waited for Jesus to step into the tomb, but instead He raised His voice: "Lazarus, come out!"

A moment passed. Then another. When a linen-wrapped

shape appeared in the mouth of the cave, there was a collective gasp. Somehow that decaying body had received life. Somehow that shell of the person who used to be known as Lazarus became Lazarus again. What had died lived even though it had died—pretty much exactly as Jesus said.

The story played to mixed reviews. Many believed in Jesus after this, including some of the religious leaders who had been antagonistic toward him. But many did not. And as word spread, controversy followed. Those with religious power found Jesus to be a formidable threat. They couldn't just let a guy run around the countryside raising people from the dead, after all. So they decided, as anyone obviously would, that in response to this audacious act of resurrection they would have to have Him killed. The irony is incredible. Jesus had brought wholeness and restoration in word and in deed, and the religious response was to consider ways to assassinate Him.

I thought about this story as I wandered among the remains of the mega-ministry. I thought about the places in my own heart that were ruins in need of restoration. And I wondered if Jesus were playing to mixed reviews in me as well. I couldn't conceive of assassinating Jesus, but I have found plenty of ways to diminish His words and engagement in my life. Can what has died in me live even though it has died? Is that the plot behind the story here? Why do I continue to believe that most of the restorative power of Jesus is something I will experience only when I no longer inhabit a human body? Jesus dispensed heavenly gifts with the touch of a human hand and called forth life with a human voice—so maybe there is a considerable amount of wholeness, restoration, and renewal available in the here and now that I've simply explained away and deferred to a point beyond my humanity.

In Lazarus's story, restoration was at hand, and all any of the people had to do was believe. I wonder if I'm not repeating the same story in my life. Maybe we all are. Maybe it doesn't have to be this way if we would just believe Him. Maybe we are settling for a human story that is full of impossibility and limitation when Jesus saw a restored humanity full of possibility and renewal.

What places in your heart are in ruins? What has died because you were abused? What is decaying because you were betrayed? What is rotting because life has simply beaten to death the person you once were? Jesus is looking into your heart and inviting you to "open it up." He is asking you to roll away the stone. He is calling your name and saying, "Come out!"

Will you believe Him? Or, like Martha, will you sidestep the disruption?

If Jesus is who He says He is, there is life in the places we thought were dead—the places that once were filled with life but are now ruins. He really does redeem everything He touches. If we just believe Him, we'll see something miraculously normal—wholeness and restoration—because He has come that we might have life.[6]

09

Rinse

On blessings, happiness, and feet

Truth, like gold, is to be obtained not by its growth,
but by washing away from it all that is not gold.

LEO TOLSTOY

THE SANDSTORM BLEW IN FROM SAUDI ARABIA and blanketed the hills. Rising like a portent of doom thousands of feet in the air, the sand was thick enough to have a flavor and tiny enough to irritate my eyes. I squinted as I stood atop the Mount of Olives and looked through the haze at the holy city of Jerusalem. Jesus once stood near where my feet were planted, and I considered how conflicted the city makes me feel inside. Clouds of tension seem to hover over Jerusalem even on a blue-sky day. God placed His name over this city, and everyone seems to want a piece of it. Everyone wants the magic, but I have wondered at times if God is even within hailing distance anymore. So many believe that everything would be right with the world if they could just control Jerusalem. They think that happiness, blessing, and fulfillment would arrive if those who were of another tribe could finally be banished. The same kinds of tension hovered over the holy city when Jesus was here, and it made Him very sad. It also got Him killed.

Most people want to be happy and blessed and are willing to fight for control—a lot like those battling for the heart of the holy city. Finding contentment and fulfillment is something we dedicate a significant portion of our lives to. Happiness is one of our driving forces. When it gets thwarted, we can get pretty focused—if not obsessive—in trying to move things back toward our own versions of happy. Sometimes we even believe we have the liberty to remove anything or anyone that interferes with our happiness. We have rights, after all.

The concepts of being known by our love or loving our neighbors as ourselves or turning the other cheek doesn't always coincide with our attempts to be happy and blessed. Hardship and challenge aren't usually things we coexist with very well. And no matter how blessed or happy we try to become, we still find that we must live within the sandstorm of our own choices.

When we juxtapose Jesus' thoughts about happiness and blessing with our own pursuits of those things, we're confronted with the fact that we may be charting a course that cannot deliver happiness at all.

In John's Gospel we find an account of the final meal Jesus had as a free man, in that same tense city of Jerusalem. Even though the weight of the world must have been on Jesus' shoulders, His posture toward his friends was beautiful.

As the meal progressed, Jesus did a most unusual and frankly awkward thing.[1] Rising to His feet, He disrobed and tied a towel around His waist. While His friends looked on, He poured a basin full of fresh water and walked into the middle of the room, where He got down on His knees.

Amusement must have been as thick as the confusion among them. This was their rabbi. Their master. They believed Him to be the Messiah and a Heaven-sent King. Kings don't get down on their knees before anyone. But here He was.

A seat-squirming discomfort probably fell over the room when He grabbed the first man's foot and placed it in the basin. Imagine the fidgeting and nervous clearing of throats as Jesus scrubbed grime from feet, ankles, and shins. The embarrassment peaked when He reached Simon Peter.

"There is no way I'm letting you wash my feet," Peter told Jesus.

Jesus smiled as He looked up. "Well, Peter," He said, "it's up to you. But if you don't let Me do this for you, you'll not only miss out on what's happening here right now, but you also won't have any place with Me."

When Jesus put it in those terms, Peter quickly changed

his mind—and moved toward the other extreme, as he was prone to do. Peter basically asked Jesus to give him a bath.

Jesus just kept rinsing.

"You've already had a bath, Peter," He said. "It's just your feet that are dirty."

There's a remarkable beauty, tension, and humanity woven into the fabric of this story. Why was Jesus doing this? What was He trying to show them in this most humbling and awkward moment?

Most of us use our feet every day. Even in a society where we have personal transportation, we still need our feet to get from one place to another. And in first-century Jewish culture, it wasn't possible to hop on a bike or jump in a car. A donkey's back or a cart was the best one could hope for. Nearly everyone walked where they needed to go, and often the journey took hours or even days. I can only imagine the condition of a person's feet after they'd been walking in sandals along a dirt trail on a hot day. Their feet would have been caked with grime, sweat, and dust.

And in this story we find the King of kings down on His knees, in His underwear, washing His friends' smelly, filthy feet. The Son of the sovereign God bowed before His creation, humbling Himself and washing away the filth of where they'd been.

Once He'd washed every foot in the room, Jesus would have been filthy Himself. It would have been a bit disgusting, to be honest. Jesus wore the grime of a dozen men's sweaty, smelly feet. The scene is very human—and very unsanitary.

He had dirt and sweat and the bacteria from between their toes splashed all over Him, but He kept rinsing until the last foot was clean. Only then did He stand and put His robe back on. And as He wiped His hands dry with a towel, He asked a cryptic question:

"Do you know what I've done for you just now?"

There isn't an obvious answer to this very human question. What He had done contained so many nuances and overtones. It was physical and sensory and humbling and open. It was an act of love and a profound and unforgettable moment of teaching. It drew their friendship deeper while opening their hearts to Jesus and one another. It spoke of the posture of the heavenly Kingdom Jesus continually spoke of.

Then Jesus answered His own complex question:

"You call me 'Teacher' and 'Lord,'" He said, "and that's correct. It's what I am. So now that I, your Lord and Teacher, have washed your feet, you should do the same thing for each other. I've given you an example that you should follow. No servant is greater than their master. So now that you know this, you will be happy and blessed if you do it."

You will be happy and blessed if you do it? *This* is how we find happiness and fulfillment? It's so simple—and so complicated.

In this act of humility, Jesus reframed some of the major motivations of our lives and how we attempt to achieve them. This works against so much of what has been ingrained in us. Blessing is supposed to be something we have to cultivate and fight for. Happiness is supposed to be something we can achieve or buy. We're indoctrinated to believe that if we could just use the right shampoo and toothpaste and then drive the right car and live in the right neighborhood and watch the right television, we should be happy. But happiness—no matter how hard we try to follow this model—becomes the carrot perpetually dangling in front of us. Every once in a while we snag a taste, but we never stop reaching for it.

Jesus was saying that all of the effort isn't going to get us there. The path to happiness, apparently, can be found by following His very unusual example: humbling ourselves enough to rinse the dust from the feet of our brothers and sisters. We find this posture in letting go of offenses, asking forgiveness, and showing kindness without conditions. In bringing comfort and release to our brothers and sisters, we wash away the filth and exhaustion they may find themselves in.

From a practical perspective, the possibilities are limitless. We can offer words of comfort or offer nothing more than our undivided attention. We can empty our pockets of loose change instead of walking by another human lost in a life of addiction. We can say the right thing instead of the wrong one. We can forgive without expecting anything in return. There is no limit to the good we can do on any given day if we're simply deliberate and aware. The posture of heart is entirely simple—love your neighbor as you love yourself. It's simple, but it requires awareness and vigilance. But in this intentionality, our true humanity shines.

Above all, we need to stop condemning one another. We often get so bogged down in trying to be superior that we forget who the Judge will be. We lose God inside our intricate belief system. We often ostracize those we disagree with or marginalize those we fear. We forget that they, like us, are made in the image of God.

We cannot be Christ-like if we act differently from Jesus. Jesus moved toward people, not away. He moved to the heart of the story and didn't get lost in the details. Jesus humbled Himself even to the point of death.[2] Our heart's posture should say, *We've already had a bath. It's just our feet that are dirty.*

All of the stuff we've accumulated will not make us happy. The illusion of blessing cannot fill the void within us. All of our search for meaning and significance won't do it either. There are things we will never know, and we can never find significance in comparison.

Jesus showed us that happiness and fulfillment can be found only in true humanity—and true humanity approaches the broken with a humble heart, washing from their lives the filth and grime of where they've been. Let's release one another from our pasts and let go of what we've been holding on to. Every day is a fresh start with God.[3] He is holding nothing back from us and nothing against us. We must do the same for each other. And if we're willing to get ourselves dirty so that others may be clean, as the Master has done for us, we will find happiness and blessing from God.

10.

Eucharist

On the bittersweet, death, and hope

Our sweetest songs are those that tell of saddest thought.

PERCY BYSSHE SHELLEY, "TO A SKYLARK"

"THE SUN OUTSHINES REGRET," he sang. The soft strum
of a beat-up acoustic guitar filled in the empty spaces. "Thank
God for metaphors 'cause it's cold here."[1]

The song was called "Hope," and it has lingered with me
in the fifteen years since my friend Paul first sang it to me.
The haunting words and melody wash over me now just as
when I listened to them for the first time.

The best songs are the ones that make you forget you're
listening to music. They do an end run around your intellect
and invade your heart with something true. Paul's song is like
that. It leaves you reaching for what you can't quite touch,
but you know is there. It's bittersweet.

Bittersweet moments encapsulate the entire story of what came before, and afterward nothing will ever be the same. Like the last breakfast before your son leaves for active combat duty in a distant land, or the night before your daughter gets married. Every remembrance that has brought you to this place comes like a torrent, and you hold on so it won't evaporate into the mist of the past. But the thing about bittersweet moments is that we can't fully live in the beauty of the sweet, because the bitterness is part of it.

I imagine Jesus must have experienced this kind of bittersweet moment as He sat to share His last supper with His friends. That time together held within it many dusty miles, the humbling beauty of God at work, the laughter, the ache of a story that was reaching its conclusion. Nothing would ever be the same for any of them after that meal, and Jesus knew it.

But I'm getting ahead of myself.

Before we get to the table, we must start in a little fishing village called Capernaum on the northwest shore of the Sea of Galilee, where Jesus made His adult home. In Capernaum, Jesus ate food. He laughed and visited with friends. He went for walks. He drank wine. He built things. He looked upon the stars through the firelight. In Capernaum, Jesus sneezed.

Remember, Jesus didn't spend His life floating six inches above the earth, aloof, detached, and completely distracted by a halo. He was fully present in the experiences and emotions of humanity. So imagine how He would have felt that day He woke up, got up off His straw sleeping mat, and realized He was about to leave Capernaum and walk, arms outstretched, toward death.

Imagine how you would feel if you woke up tomorrow morning and realized that you would never be coming home again alive. That everything was about to change for the life you'd known and the people you loved.

Now we're getting into the real story.

The walk Jesus was about to take was a long one and mostly uphill. It wasn't the first time He'd taken this journey, but this time He knew that the end of the journey meant death. As His friends laughed and joked around Him, He felt the weight of knowing that every forward step took Him closer to unspeakable suffering. Can you imagine the melancholy in that? The loneliness?

Jesus' life on earth was full of showing us what normal humanity was meant to be—what a normal human was meant to be. But as He walked toward His death, He began to do something more. We think that Jesus' death was about shouldering our sin—and it was. But Jesus' life was also about shouldering the pain of our inhumanity, the pain of our loneliness and relational detachment, the bitter that overcomes the sweet. He took those things—the deepest hurts and brokenness of humanity—and carried those to the cross. Because humanity itself could not be restored without the death of everything that made it subhuman.

According to the Gospel narratives, Jesus became very intentional with His words as He and His friends walked the ancient paths that led toward the holy city of Jerusalem, trying to warn the disciples of what was about to happen. But they didn't understand. It's easy enough to assume the disciples were backward or totally unaware as they followed Jesus, and in some ways they were. But perhaps this assumption isn't really fair. The disciples had a worldview just as we do, and like many of the people who followed Jesus around, they believed the Messiah was going to inspire people to revolt against the Roman occupiers of the day. For them, the Kingdom of Heaven Jesus had been talking about was not just a spiritual place but also a very human one—one that would include the restoration of Jerusalem to God. So when Jesus said He would suffer and be taken from them, His words didn't exactly compute.

As Jesus carried the heaviness of what awaited Him, we see how out of step and unaware His friends were. James and John privately approached Jesus to ask that they be given seats on His right and left hand when He came into His Kingdom—a throne they were expecting Him to mount in Jerusalem.[2] They thought that this journey to Jerusalem was a mighty move of God, that the Messiah would finally be revealed—and they were right. But it wouldn't be anything like they thought. And being so misunderstood by His closest friends must have only added to Jesus' feelings of isolation.

We all know what it feels like to have those we love misunderstand us. We've been in those conversations with a spouse or a friend where we feel as if we are speaking different languages. We each understand what isolation feels like.

None of these things were meant to be a part of our human experience. And in recognizing that Jesus also experienced these things, we encounter something fascinating: If Jesus is God, as we believe Him to be, then everything Jesus experienced is something God was willing to experience personally. God was willing to experience the inhumanity we chose in order to draw us back into the humanity He created.

But let's move back into the story.

The strenuous climb out of the Judean desert up toward Jerusalem was physically exhausting, but eventually they crested the Mount of Olives to see all of Jerusalem spread out before them. The city was alive with the festivities of Passover. Tens of thousands of pilgrims had flooded in to take part in the celebration. The disciples were beyond excited, but Jesus must have felt a cold chill as He looked upon the Temple—His Temple. His creation had completely misunderstood God in the flesh.

As the excitement of His arrival began to draw a crowd, Jesus sent His friends to find a colt. The people hailed Him as the King, throwing palm branches before Him and shouting words of adoration and joy.[3]

Jesus' followers still, of course, had a completely different understanding of what was happening. They thought the main event had begun.

At this point, Jesus was emotionally shattered. He alone saw what was happening. His heart broke over Jerusalem—and Jerusalem was about to break Him completely.

"How I wish today that you of all people would understand

the way to peace. But now it is too late, and peace is hidden from your eyes," He said, weeping.[4]

His emotional outpouring must have felt out of sync with the celebration that was taking place, but this is how we arrive in the upper room for the Last Supper. Both the location and the event have become iconic to the faith, but in the midst of mythologizing and philosophizing, perhaps we've lost its breathtaking humanity.

Jesus and His friends met not in a gilded holy place filled with smoke and translucent angels, but in the spare room of a friend's home. And it wasn't the grand and glorious occasion we so often picture: It was, very simply, a meal that happened to be Jesus' last. It was the last time He would be together with His friends to remember all they'd been through together.

The scene is profoundly bittersweet in its rich relationship mingled with the painful expectation of what's to come. Imagine you've gathered your closest friends and family together for a dinner because you're about to have an experimental surgery that you have a 2 percent chance of surviving, and you'll understand a bit of the human emotion Jesus felt as He sat down to this meal.

Jesus smiled, though He carried an unbelievable emotional and spiritual weight on His shoulders. He told His friends how much He'd been looking forward to their meal together.[5] It was a celebration of all that had been—a remarkable memorial to the fact that God came to earth in person to involve Himself in humanity. Jesus broke the bread and passed the cup and told them never to forget that moment and all it represented. He knew they were going to need the reminder later. What was about to happen was going to shake everything they thought they knew about God. And He knew we'd all need it even today.

What we witness in this supper is the last time things would feel safe and normal for any of these men. In a couple of hours, the bonds that held them would be blown apart. This one meal, in the comfort and privacy of this upper room, was the last moment of common serenity in their lives. They were about to experience the full force of inhumanity. And it was during this meal that, as we know, Jesus got down on His knees before His friends and washed their feet—one more taste of what humanity was meant to be.

After the meal, Jesus crossed the Kidron Valley and wandered a little way up the slope of the Mount of Olives to a grove of trees known as Gethsemane. He gathered His closest friends nearby for moral support—but they fell asleep. It seems they had no clear understanding of the emotional load Jesus was carrying, just as they did not anticipate the momentous events soon to take place.

Jesus was in such emotional distress and agony of spirit that He was sweating profusely.[6] The emotional torture— and the essence of broken humanity—was very real.

"Is there any way you can get me out of this?" He cried to the Father. "I would prefer this cup to pass me by."[7] It's a prayer we've all probably prayed a thousand times. But although Jesus prayed for an alternative path, He was committed to following through with whatever God was setting before Him.

It wasn't long before a mob entered among the olive trees, searching for Jesus. They were, of course, led by one of Jesus' closest friends—one who had just enjoyed the final meal with Him. Jesus felt the cold, black kiss of betrayal as Judas's lips brushed His face. He felt the ropes and chains wrap around Him as His freedom was taken. He heard the racing footsteps of the last of His friends as they abandoned Him. Jesus was completely and utterly alone.

What makes this scene so moving and tragic is that we probably each have stories of betrayal, isolation, and abandonment. We know to some degree what this feels like. And this is our God we're speaking of—a human God abandoned, betrayed, and isolated by those He created.

Jesus was dragged back across the Kidron Valley into the quarters of the high priest, where all sorts of accusations were hurled at Him. He was smacked around, spit upon, and abused for hours before He was lowered into a dungeon while His captors hatched a deal to take Him before the Roman authorities.

The ruins of the high priest's quarters still remain in Jerusalem, and as with many places associated with Jesus, they have been venerated as holy over the millennia. A beautiful and contemplative chapel stands there today, but as with much of history, the truth is beneath the ground. It's possible even today to descend beneath the church of St. Peter in

Gallicantu into the cisterns and caves of the first century that were used for storing things like water, supplies—and people.

Jesus would have probably been lowered by a rope tied around His wrists into one of these pits. The rope would have been tied off with little slack so that He couldn't lie down and rest. Exhausted from emotional exertion and verbal abuse, He would have had little to think about aside from what was coming next for Him—which was unthinkable.

I've stood in these caves many times. They have become a place of great personal meaning to me. I love them for what they represent, but they're also some of the places I hate most on the face of the earth. Jesus has become my best friend. He's my closest ally in life. He's my Savior. I can barely stand to think of Him in a place like that.

As Jesus was enduring the trauma of this terrible evening, one of His best friends, Peter, was in the courtyard of the high priest's complex, denying that he even knew who Jesus was. Often we think of Jesus' going before the council of accusers as a separate event from Peter's denial, but in reality there was only a wall that separated Peter from Jesus. Alone and exhausted in an empty cistern, Jesus could have heard Peter's denials with His own ears. Peter and Jesus were not physically far from each other. But they were worlds apart.

Under the cover of darkness, the rest of Jesus' friends remained hidden. They were watching. They still believed He was the coming Messiah, so they must have thought that something big was about to happen. What was taking place didn't make a lot of sense to them, but Jesus had never let them down. They were ready to join in a great revolt. But what happened next would be impossibly confusing and heart-wrenching for them.

Nothing could have prepared their hearts for the bitter ashes of defeat. Nothing could have prepared their eyes for the things they would never be able to unsee. Nothing could have readied them for the crimson loss they would feel or the complete vertigo of a world shifting uncontrollably beneath their feet.

They had trusted Judas. He was their brother. And to betray Jesus with a kiss—the very symbol of loyalty and trust—was unspeakable and utterly unforgivable. In a profound irony, the last of Jesus' followers to be near Him before He walked toward a cross *was* Judas. It's almost poetically fitting: The journey toward the cross was for people like Judas—people like you and me.

As I write about this betrayal and abandonment, my heart reaches in empathy toward Jesus. Doesn't yours? When Jesus was ridiculed and smacked, He felt it. When His beard was grabbed and yanked, it hurt. The spit dripping down His cheek had literally come from someone's mouth, and the lies shrieked into His face were as lacerations to His soul.

God's visit to earth had revealed a humanity that humanity wasn't ready to accept or tolerate. The perfect humanity that Jesus lived and told them about contrasted so starkly with the tangled web of life as they knew it. The religious powers determined that His teachings were unachievable fairy tales and heresies and that Jesus Himself was a blasphemer.

In their minds, leaving that kind of message in the hands of a gifted communicator would have been a dangerous and drastic miscalculation. After all, the peasants would follow anyone.

In some ways it's easy to see where they were coming from. For them to believe that Jesus was divine would be like us believing that David Koresh or Jim Jones were God. It just didn't compute. They could not see that the invitation Jesus was offering them as anything but unrealistic. He could not bring about the victory they were hoping for. And whatever Kingdom He was talking about seemed neither real nor realistic. What they could see was how He constantly uncovered their dark inner workings. The truth could have liberated them, but they didn't really want to face it because Jesus was not the Messiah they sought. They decided it was better for one man to die than for His ideas to unsettle the tenuous power distribution they had so carefully constructed.

If I'm honest, I can't say that I wouldn't have been in the crowd calling for Jesus' crucifixion. I don't know. It's clear in the Gospels that a few days before, people—probably many of the same people—were hailing Jesus as the new King. I have no idea what the pull of that culture or the fear of standing counter to the mob might have been like. I would probably have been hiding like the disciples, completely misreading the revolution and redemption that was taking place among the human species.

I'd like to think that I wouldn't abandon Jesus in the garden of Gethsemane either, but I'm no different from the disciples. This bothers me greatly because I really love Jesus. My hopes and aspirations are wrapped around Him. But I don't know that I'd be any different. It shows me the depth of my own gasping struggle to live into the humanity Jesus offers and the constant battle that exists for my heart.

———

In the face of the worst that broken humanity had to offer, Jesus continued to live from a fully and truly human place. As He endured unending interrogation intended to break Him down, Jesus did not flood the room with words in His own defense as most of us would under the same circumstances. He knew who He was. And He knew what He was doing.

In our modern world, criminal investigations and trials are often incredibly detailed and lengthy. But Jesus' world was very different—the investigation was hasty, His trial over quickly. Clearly, justice was not the motive. One system of power used another to get a quick judgment—one that would leave an innocent man hanging naked on a cross.

The fact that Jesus said very little in the interrogations was actually quite compelling—especially to the Roman prefect Pontius Pilate. He was used to blubbering pleas for mercy or defiance from hardened mercenaries. Jesus was different.[8]

"Your friends tell me you're a king. Is that true? Are you the King of the Jews?" Pilate asked.

Jesus replied, "If that's what you say."

Pilate's eyebrows rose. Was this man being sarcastic? He looked long at Jesus. The corners of his mouth began to rise into a smirk of understanding. This man wasn't a problem—He was just a harmless, delusional peasant from some backwater village.

"I don't see a problem with this man," Pilate said. And after discovering that Jesus was from Galilee, he shipped Him across the palace complex to Herod Antipas, who had jurisdiction over that region.

Herod was excited. He'd been hearing the stories about Jesus. He wanted to see the magic. But Jesus stood completely mute before him. He could have done something. He could have made His move, and everyone would have followed Him. But this was not the mission. Proving His power was not His objective. Restoring humanity's equilibrium was.

Herod fired question after question at Jesus while the religious leaders hurled accusations from the sidelines. Jesus just stood there. He didn't say a word.

Herod came to the same conclusion Pilate had. Jesus might have been crazy, but He wasn't a problem.

To send a little humor Pilate's way, Herod told his men to drape Jesus in a royal robe, insinuating that he had found this deluded commoner to in fact be the King of the Jews. Pilate liked the joke. Pilate and Herod (who had been enemies before this) became friends that day.[9]

Pilate met with the Jewish council and explained that he and Herod had reached identical conclusions about this man Jesus: Whatever He was, He wasn't leading a terrorist rebellion and wasn't a problem as far as the empire was concerned.

The eruption of the mob was enormous and startling.

Pilate began to realize that this wasn't about justice. It was a vendetta. They wanted this man's blood. Jesus was clearly innocent, but the crowd wanted Him dead.

Pilate had intended to serve justice fairly, but the people didn't want justice. They wanted blood. The tug-of-war in Pilate's mind swayed in their favor. Did he really want to risk riots over a delusional peasant? Who cared? Jesus wasn't a Roman citizen.

Pilate washed his hands in front of the crowd, letting them know that this was not the Roman way. The Romans had no problem punishing the guilty, but this was not a matter of true justice.

The orders were issued, and Jesus was punished severely at a whipping post. His human skin was torn from head to foot by tiny lead balls and fragments of bone attached to multistranded leather straps. The blinding agony from every frayed human nerve would have been an excruciating hell. Then, overwhelmed by exhaustion and blood loss, Jesus was forced to carry the beam that His body would be attached to.

Jesus stumbled His way out of the Roman military outpost, and the soldiers and crowds herded Him outside the city walls and onto a well-trodden hill. This was to be an extremely public humiliation.

He was stripped and held stationary by a practiced execution crew. With efficiency and indifference, they hammered nails through His wrists and feet. Gasps and blood sputtered from Jesus' lips. The soldiers raised the cross so that all passersby might bear witness to the awful price of rebellion against Rome. Never mind that rebellion was not the cause of this scene.

The crucifixion of Jesus Christ has arrested the attention of billions of people, beginning on the day it happened. Approaching the Crucifixion with indifference is nearly impossible. The scene is so powerfully compelling that no matter what we believe about Jesus, we can hardly look away.

The reality of Jesus' beating and crucifixion is reprehensibly brutal. The torture of the cross left Him panting for air, trying to keep from suffocating while enduring gruesome agony from the nails driven through His wrists and ankles.

How does a person defend humanity before God in a scene like this? The Crucifixion was impossibly shocking and inhumane. But perhaps that is exactly the point. To declare something inhumane is to acknowledge that it lacks humanity—it's not human. Everything about the Cross—the pain, the horror, the ache and relational brokenness leading up to it—is not what God created humanity to be.

Think about the suffering we see in the world. It's not human—and it's not God who is doing the damage. Rather, God came to undo it. Humanity slides only toward inhumanity when it remains separated from its created state of being utterly dependent on and intertwined with God. And the Crucifixion highlights just how far humanity—every one of us—has fallen.

But we know this. It's the heart of the Christian faith.

Our degenerate state was incurable.[10] We were separated

from God—humanity was separated from divinity.[11] With no way to restore the breach, we were not only doomed but damned to an inhuman and subhuman existence apart from God.[12] We were condemned to pain, to brokenness, to sin, to death. But then God invaded the earth and came as one of us.[13] His life revealed what people were created to look and act like.[14] His message was of a Kingdom that is in and among us.[15] His death spanned the chasm that our human depravity had caused, and it restored us.[16] When we accept the offer of the gospel, we die to who we were—inhuman, fallen, devolved, without God—and are resurrected as new creatures.[17] We are reborn with the divine and the human reintegrated as it was always intended because Christ now lives within us.[18] It is His divine nature within us that rescues our eternity and reclaims our humanity.[19]

The roadmap of our faith is also the roadmap of our humanity. Disconnected from God within us, we become inhuman. We have no idea what we're doing. And perhaps this is what we see playing out on the Cross.

Jesus asked the Father to forgive the people who were killing Him because they didn't know what they were doing.[20] And we are the same: Apart from God we don't know what we're doing. Apart from God we can do nothing.[21] Apart from God we are less than we were created to be. But again, we already know this. Let's put new words next to the old:

Apart from God we are less than human.

Jesus knows this. And He has compassion on us all. In offering forgiveness to the very people who were in the process of killing Him, Jesus illustrated the posture of what true humanity is supposed to look like—faith, hope, and love to the very end and beyond.

But what about justice? Are we to just take whatever is dished out and smile? No. But the fully-realized humanity Jesus taught and lived is a place of complete shalom—the peace and order of God at all times, in all places, and in all things. In this place—where humanity is as it was created—justice is constant and normal. Acts of inhumanity cease. Immediate reconciliation is the status quo.

Doesn't this all sound idealistic and esoteric? As if I'm coming to some wild view of an impossible life? This is how Jesus' detractors looked at His life and message—and they killed Him for it. We need to be careful that our hearts choose a different path.

The words Jesus spoke at His last were of utter dependence on His Father. He died the way He had lived.

"Into Your hands I surrender My Spirit," He said.[22]

These words are stunningly beautiful, but they also contain a profound truth: Death is the great equalizer for each of us. No matter what we do or do not believe, the moment of death is a leap of faith. If I jump off a diving board, what I believe or how I've acted doesn't matter: I'm certainly going to splash into the water below. Even if we don't believe in God or an afterlife, we still have to take a leap of faith and hope we're not wrong. For a Christ follower, the end of life requires our absolute trust in God. It's as if our whole faith journey leads us to one final step of faith. Jesus had to take that step too. And until we realize how utterly dependent on God we really are, we will never become like Jesus.

Jesus put Himself in an impossible situation. After all, what is more impossible or final than death?

Although, as it turns out, death is not as final as we might have thought.

I don't know the story that has brought you to this page. But since you're human, you've probably dealt with the effects of inhumanity at some point. No doubt your story is full of the bitter and the bittersweet. We linger in the pain and isolation because there seems to be no other way—no other hope for something else. And we'll even believe that God has abandoned us or simply doesn't understand at all what we're going through. And yet, Jesus' death tells us otherwise. He carried the deepest rejection, pain, and heartache with Him all the way to the Cross, taking the broken pieces of our humanity to die with the rebellion that brought us to this place.

Jesus knew loneliness. He also knew isolation. He understood what it was like to be misunderstood. He knew abandonment. He knew betrayal. He knew verbal abuse. He even knew brutal physical abuse, torture, and death. In truth, Jesus intimately understands every single human emotion and experience because He was one of us. And that's a surprising and overpowering reality. Because if Jesus is God, then God absolutely does know exactly what you're going through right now because He's experienced it firsthand.

Through His death, Jesus has restored our humanity, but we still live in an inhuman world. There is a longing, pure and true, in the depths of our identity that constantly reaches for wholeness and restoration—for the way things ought to be. And as this longing boils down to its essential core, we find what we need—hope. One day all will be restored, and we have a part to play in that redemption.

Sneezing Jesus

On infectious, chronic, terminal love

I look up to heaven only when I want to sneeze.

IVAN TURGENEV, *Fathers and Sons*

WE START, AS WE MUST, in a dark tomb of hewn stone. Jesus' corpse lay tightly wrapped, His blood congealing as his lifeless body cooled. His eyes stared blankly at nothing. His skin was pallid and His lips were blue. He was dead. Inhumanity had overcome humanity once again—or so it seemed.

But we do not end there.

Because three days later, everything changed. His pulse returned. Breath filled His lungs. And Jesus opened His eyes.

The Resurrection must have been an amazing human experience. Obviously, I do not know what resurrection feels like physically. But I imagine it to be a pleasant if shocking sensation. And while I don't know what it's like, I will.[1]

Isn't that the hope? And isn't that the final illustration Jesus was portraying with His human life? That nothing is impossible when a human life is intertwined with the divine life of God?

Jesus entrusted Himself to the impossible: that suffering would not break Him and that death would not hold Him. There is no darkness that He fears. No brokenness He won't breach. No life He didn't give His life to reclaim. No pain He cannot relate to. He entered death and came back with life. And He offers that same life to all who believe. This life Jesus offers is what we were intended to be.

To become who we were created to be, we must allow the divine life of the risen and fearless Christ within to make impossible situations possible. We must be able to stare into the face of darkness with stone-cold resolve: Death must and will yield. Which isn't to say that nothing will be difficult. It's a long, hard battle to pull a species forward to the way it was created, and we are smack in the middle of the fight.

But we aren't alone. Jesus didn't stay dead, and He's never been absent. In fact, everything He did following His resurrection was to help His followers—and us—understand just how present He is, even if it's in ways we don't typically understand. Think about His interactions with the disciples in the days before His ascension. He would show up in places unexpectedly and would withdraw just as unexpectedly. He was almost playful—appearing and then disappearing again. It's as if He were becoming less present to His disciples—but as they would learn, He was actually becoming more present.

He was teaching them a greater lesson on what it would mean to remain in His presence.

After the Resurrection, His presence was more than His physical being—far more. Now that the victory had been won, the human and the divine were being reintegrated as God had always intended. Jesus was showing them that they could never be separated—even if He physically disappeared—because He had become a part of who they were.[2] It is a state of being we all must awaken to.

For thirty-three years Jesus had breathed the air and roamed the countryside. He had lived a fully human life—but it was time to return to the Father. He and His friends walked out of Jerusalem and back up the Mount of Olives—the same slope that brought Jesus into Jerusalem in the first place. He shared His final moments with them. They had a final conversation. He told them that He had accomplished what He came to do—that all authority in Heaven and on earth had been given to Him. The entire identity of the human race had been changed forever. Humanity was no longer separated but restored to God. Humanity as it was created to be was possible again. And then Jesus told them to go tell everyone this Good News.

Or to put it another way . . . to sneeze.

───────

When you think about it, a sneeze is entirely fascinating. Imagine a two-liter bottle filled three-quarters with soda, and then imagine the soda to be air. This is the approximate volume expelled in a sneeze. Up to forty thousand droplets of saliva rocket out of the nose and mouth as fast as one hundred miles per hour. One hundred thousand germs can be expelled in a single sneeze, and if the sneezer is sick, as many as two hundred million tiny virus particles are propelled into the air. They can survive, squirming and contagious, for hours or even days, depending on where they land. A five-foot blast zone leaves a cloud of airborne particles that can descend like an invisible fog and travel through an entire room.

From a social perspective, the completely normal sneeze has invited cosmic interpretation for a very long time. Ancient Greeks thought a sneeze was a prophetic sign from the gods. Even today, the Greeks think that a sneeze solidifies as true whatever was spoken just prior to the sneeze. In many other countries, people believe a sneeze indicates that someone is thinking about you. We say all sorts of things to a person who has sneezed, and most of them seem to invoke God and His involvement in some way: "God bless you," "May you live long," "May God have mercy on you."

Everyone sneezes. It's a normal, human occurrence. And when you think about it, we're all sneezing something. Spiritually we're either expelling the Good News of Kingdom humanity or spreading the disease of inhumanity. So what if we were sneezing Jesus? What if the presence of the risen Savior were the residue we left behind—a trail of love that infected everyone?

More than two billion people alive on this planet believe

that Jesus is the Savior—nearly a third of the earth's population. We are already larger than any other kingdom on the face of the earth. What if we really were known by our love and not by the stereotypes? What if we became authentically infected with the love of Christ? What kind of influence would we have if we were sneezing a pure and true Jesus who was vibrant and alive within us and not just a mythical superhero?

According to Jesus, it would be like leaven in a loaf of rising bread. No one would be able to point to a specific person or incident, but things would start to change everywhere—the loaf would rise. The evidence of the Kingdom would be undeniable. Think of it: the world infected with the love of the risen Christ in and among us. It could become an epidemic. It could wreak havoc on the darkness. Injustice would fade into memory. Lack would be overwhelmed in an onslaught of mercy. Fear would wilt in the face of exposure to the life of Christ within.

I know this all sounds idealistic. I get it. But we can't escape the fact that this didn't seem to be idealistic to Jesus. It's how He saw things, and it's what He saw in us. Upon His ascension, He put the world back in our hands with His authority to back it up. We certainly have to put our trust in Jesus, but Jesus has put His trust in us. This is how relationships are shaped. The baton is in our hands. We will be the ones to demonstrate whether or not there is true love between Jesus and ourselves. He's already done His part and continues to love us wholeheartedly with every breath we take.

We have to take to heart what we see all around us. The battle between darkness and light is everywhere. News of the Kingdom is everywhere, if we'll pay attention and celebrate the essentials of our faith while offering grace and mercy in our differences. Life is such a ferocious opponent of death, even though death sometimes feels like it's got the upper hand.

At a recent gathering in Colorado to honor a hero in the faith, death was described as a "mockery." And that feels right, doesn't it? Darkness and death are such a mockery of us and who we were created to be. Death is most literally a crime against humanity. But the Scriptures tell us, "That is why we never give up. Though our bodies are dying, our spirits are being renewed every day."[3]

This renewal doesn't begin when we die. It's right now and every day. Every day is a choice to participate in sanctification—both in our spirits and in the world.

We have to be Jesus in this world, and again this is not a metaphor. We have to get about the business of saving the world. I realize that we can hardly save anyone from his or her sins. But we can sure put a dent in suffocating the darkness.

I've heard it said that success amounts to moving in the same direction for a long time with a specific goal in mind. Much more wholeness is available to our humanity. Do you want it badly enough to contend for it—to move in the same direction for a long time with wholeness as the goal? Because wholeness is what Jesus looked like.

Wholeness is Christ-like.

And we've been living fragmented too long—generations too long.

There is an elegant completeness in a person who is as they were created to be. They are a seamless transition between the physical and spiritual—and between the human and the divine. The only person I know who demonstrates this is Jesus. This is what Jesus lived to reveal to us and died to offer us. We can be much more whole than we are.

Not long ago I was watching the film *A Story Worth Living* with my sons. The film concludes with everyone enjoying a lovely Colorado evening at twilight. The characters sit in a circle around a fire. The discussion is about wholeness and the soul's longing for a time of complete restoration and what that might be like.

"That nothing is between me and any other person— no misunderstanding" was how one character described this wholeness. Another added, "That everything I have lost will be returned." Nods of approval and expressions of affirmation filled in the space. Then another spoke: "That nothing is lost and that there are no more good-byes."

This is *shalom*.

This is what we were made for. It is how life is supposed to be for us. This is humanity in its glory, but it waits. It cannot be while we live fallen. And perhaps it cannot fully be realized until the Savior's return—but we can have so much more right now than we might realize.

Jesus has been standing at the door and knocking for

a long time now. He's been inviting us back into a collab-orative life—a fully human life. Because Jesus didn't only rescue our souls—He rescued our humanity. Jesus isn't an insurance policy covering eternity that kicks in only after we die and our lives have been audited. Jesus is as immediate as our next breath. Humans were made for this world, and we are either infecting it with light and life or adding to the animal misery around us. And we can do better than we've been doing.

Becoming Christ-like means to become as He is. And Jesus is God, my friend. So when we're talking about becom-ing Christ-like, we're also talking about becoming God-like. That's how huge we're talking.

As we imitate Jesus and collaborate with Him, we begin to know His ways in this world. As we walk in His ways, we will begin to live as He did. If we will do this in a straight line for a long time with our whole hearts, we will be head-ing toward our created identity the entire time—we will be heading toward wholeness.

Every moment we're sneezing something, and what we're sneezing begins within our own hearts. If the Kingdom is not within us, it will never be among us. We can't sneeze a Jesus we don't really know and for whom we are not lovesick. The love of Jesus can spread like a virus, but we cannot share that which we do not possess. It starts inside us and then infects our families. We have no problem passing a cold or the flu to one another, so we should have no problem infecting one another with love, joy, peace, longsuffering, kindness, goodness, loyalty, gentleness, and self-control.[4] We all make one another sick, and we can all make one another well.

You have the power to mount a massive attack of love on everyone you care for. You can respond to violence and darkness with an attack of faith, hope, and charity. And as we infect the world with the love of Jesus, our hearts are literally being transformed and made new. We are becoming as we were intended to be.[5] We're becoming truly human.

Do you want this?

It's time to engage. Be conscious that you are sneezing something everywhere you go.

We aren't invited into a cowardly faith; we're invited to love ferociously as we surrender to the tempest that is the fierce and unstoppable love of Jesus. *This* can change the world. And this can make the impossible possible—God's will being done on earth as it is in Heaven.

Take back your heart and give it unreservedly to God. Take back your family and love without ceasing. The collaborative effect of the body of Christ rising will be the unity we long for and the change we hope in. We can bring a lovesick people to a lovesick God. May we become so infected with the resurrection power of Jesus that it is impossible to find ourselves outside of Him.

Because without Jesus we can do nothing.[6] With Him all things are possible.[7] God should be able to send us into impossible situations and make them possible for us— exactly as Jesus did.[8] Extraordinary is supposed to be ordinary. Supernatural is supposed to be natural. The divine is within the human. We must walk into darkness and replace it with light in every conceivable way. We must be able to stare through death and see that there is no end. With God we are truly human—and the possibilities are limitless.

May the Lord bless you and keep you.
May He make His face to shine upon you and
* be gracious to you.*
May He lift up His countenance on you and give
* you peace.*

May the strength of God go with you.
May the wisdom of God instruct you,
May the hand of God protect you,
May the Word of God direct you.
May you be sealed in Christ this day and forevermore.

Amen.

Acknowledgments

THE TRUTH IS that I can't believe I get to write books. And I have to start by thanking you for reading them. The three books I've published have come out of my own search for context and meaning that informs my faith journey. I'm glad I'm not alone in the search and deeply grateful that we can live into it together.

My wife, Jill, deserves untold thanks from just about every angle I can think of. I can say honestly that I wouldn't know how to do what I do without her presence in my life. A few words of public gratitude are simply not enough. I have a good wife, and writing our story with the life we have together is my greatest honor.

If there is one thing that has taught me more about the heart of Jesus toward me and toward the world, it would be my children. Tyler, Cristian, China, Maxwell, Ezekiel, and my grandson, Boston—I love you with all my heart. I seriously love everything about you.

The Daily Audio Bible community is beyond inspiring

to me. The journey we are on and the rhythm it takes in our lives as we move through the Bible together is my life's work. I love you and thank you beyond words.

To the NavPress team, I give humble gratitude for offering me a home and a platform from which to creatively explore. Don Pape, you are legendary, and there are valid reasons for this.

Thank you to Melissa Myers, Stephanie Wright, David Geeslin, Robin Bermel, Jeff Rustemeyer, and the whole team with the NavPress/Tyndale Alliance. And thank you to Dave Zimmerman for your excellent copyediting skills and insightful questions.

And Caitlyn Carlson . . . thank you. Seriously, thank you. When the words have become a blur, you put them right. This was quite the collaboration. Thank you for giving it your best.

I'd also like to thank the team at Tyndale. Thank you for a second dance.

I thank my friends and family. There are so many names—so many people I owe a debt of gratitude to, and it's so far beyond this book. My brother, Jaymey, and his wife, Lindsay; Brad; Chris; Four Winds; John and the entire team at Ransomed Heart; Mike and Jen; every church and venue all over this beautiful earth that has ever invited me to come speak; Andrew and Natalie; Tia and all the More girls; Chet and Daniel for caring for the code and making the whole thing work at Daily Audio Bible every day; Sarahjane for continuing to keep my world spinning as efficiently as it can;

Jason and Sandy; Mark and LeeAn; and everyone else—all of you. If you know me, I thank you. If you don't but have taken the *Sneezing Jesus* journey—then we know each other. Thank you.

And to Jesus. I've said the words I felt You wanted said. It was hard. Words cannot contain You. You are beautiful beyond words, and what I want more than anything is to be like You.

If you're hungry for this Jesus we've been talking about, join us at DailyAudioBible.com, where you can go through the entire Bible, read fresh every day, and you'll find a community of people the world over who are hungry for the same.

In memory of Rosalie Hardin and Craig McConnell.

Notes

PROLOGUE
1. Hebrews 2:5-18; 2 John 1:7.

CHAPTER 1: ADVENT
1. Genesis 2:7.
2. Genesis 6:5.
3. Luke 1:39-45.
4. Luke 2:7, NASB.
5. Hebrews 4:15.
6. Genesis 1:27; 2 Peter 1:3-4.

CHAPTER 2: BACKWARD
1. Matthew 5–7.
2. Matthew 5:3-11.
3. Matthew 5:20.
4. Matthew 5:21-24.
5. Matthew 6:33; Luke 12:31.
6. Matthew 10:7.
7. Matthew 13:24.
8. Matthew 13:31.
9. Matthew 13:33.
10. Matthew 13:44.
11. Matthew 13:45.
12. Matthew 13:47.
13. Matthew 22:2.
14. Luke 17:20-21.
15. Luke 1:37.
16. Luke 18:17, NIV.
17. 2 Corinthians 3:18.
18. Matthew 22:36-39; Mark 12:29-31; Luke 10:27; cf. Leviticus 19:18; Deuteronomy 6:4-5.
19. Luke 12:32, KJV.

CHAPTER 3: WEEP
1. Psalm 56:8, NLT.
2. Luke 7:39.
3. Luke 7:48, NLT.

CHAPTER 4: GO AWAY
1. Luke 8.
2. Matthew 9:8; 10:1; 28:18; Mark 3:15; 6:7; Luke 9:1; 10:19; Romans 6:4, 11; 8:2, 11, 39; 1 Corinthians 6:14; 15:28; 2 Corinthians 4:7; 6:7; Ephesians 1:10, 22; 3:19; 6:10; Philippians 3:10; Colossians 2:10, 20; 2 Timothy 1:7, 14; Hebrews 2:8; 1 Peter 3:22; Jude 1:25; Revelation 2:26-28.
3. Galatians 2:20.
4. 2 Peter 1:4.

CHAPTER 5: BETWEEN A PLACE & A HARD ROCK

1. Matthew 16; Mark 8; Luke 9.
2. 1 Corinthians 12:27.
3. Colossians 1:18.
4. Luke 17:20-21.
5. 2 Peter 1:4.

CHAPTER 6: KERATOCONUS

1. Mark 8:24, KJV.
2. John 21:25.
3. Mark 5; Luke 8.
4. Mark 10.
5. John 14:12, NLT.

CHAPTER 7: NEIGHBORS

1. Luke 10.
2. Luke 10:25, NIV.
3. Luke 10:26.
4. See Genesis 32:22-28.
5. Luke 10:27, NLT.
6. Luke 10:28.
7. Luke 10:29, NIV.
8. Matthew 25:40.

CHAPTER 8: OPEN IT UP

1. John 11.
2. John 11:35.
3. John 11:21-24.
4. John 11:33.
5. John 11:40.
6. John 10:10.

CHAPTER 9: RINSE

1. John 13.

2. Philippians 2:8.
3. Lamentations 3:22-23.

CHAPTER 10: EUCHARIST

1. Paul Alan, "Hope," unpublished work. Used with permission.
2. Matthew 20:20-21; Mark 10:35-37.
3. John 12:12-15.
4. Luke 19:42, NLT.
5. Luke 22:15.
6. Luke 22:44.
7. Luke 22:42.
8. Luke 23.
9. Luke 23:11-12.
10. Psalm 51:5; Romans 3:23.
11. Isaiah 59:2; Ephesians 2:12.
12. Romans 6:23; 7:5, 24.
13. Hebrews 2:14.
14. John 14:12; 1 John 2:6.
15. Luke 17:21.
16. Mark 10:45; John 3:16; Romans 5:10; 2 Corinthians 5:21; Galatians 3:13; 1 Peter 2:24; 1 John 2:2.
17. Romans 6:8; 2 Corinthians 5:17; Galatians 2:20; Colossians 3:3; 2 Timothy 2:11.
18. Romans 8:10; 2 Corinthians 13:5; Galatians 2:20; Ephesians 3:17; Colossians 1:27.
19. 2 Peter 1:4.

20. Luke 23:34.
21. John 15:5.
22. Luke 23:46.

CHAPTER 11: SNEEZING JESUS

1. 1 Corinthians 6:14.
2. John 17:21.
3. 2 Corinthians 4:16, NLT.
4. See Galatians 5:22-23.
5. Ezekiel 36:26; 2 Corinthians 5:17.
6. John 15:5.
7. Luke 18:27.
8. John 14:12.

DAY 1

January 1

Genesis 1:1–2:25; Matthew 1:1–2:12;
Psalm 1:1-6; Proverbs 1:1-6

Our journey begins as all must: at the start, or in the beginning. Today's reading is an important first step because knowing where we've come from gives us the context we need to rightly interpret our own life's story. "In the beginning God created the heavens and the earth," the Bible begins. And this launches us into the grand adventure that is before us. In one year, we will travel many dusty miles and meet deeply fascinating people who will become meaningful friends to us. They are our spiritual ancestors. In their stories our own hearts will be revealed.

On this first of 365 days, we see God's care and intentionality with all His creation. We learn that our human experience was fashioned in God's own image, deriving its animating life source from the breath of God Himself. It is not by chance that we exist—it is by design. You're supposed to be here. You bear the image of a God who is intertwined with your story in a way that goes deeper than cells and atoms.

Today we get an amazing and rare view of how things

were always supposed to be for us. We see a perfect world with perfect people created in God's image. And this image of perfection, contrasted with the world we currently live in, allows us a sobering look at how the story has turned over the millennia—but we'll get to that over the next few days.

The Bible is a beautiful and divinely inspired book. Embark on this journey to read it in its entirety with great anticipation, for from Genesis to Revelation the Bible tells the cohesive story of God's unwillingness to be left out of the human story—your story. And in the book of Matthew today, as we learn the details of the coming of Jesus, we read of the great lengths God was willing to go to that He might rescue His perfect creation. Meanwhile, Psalms and Proverbs will offer daily guidance, wisdom, and comfort for the issues of our everyday lives.

Together we'll be surprised by how often what we read in the Bible will be a mirror into our own hearts and motives. And we'll be delighted to understand that God is not a distant and uninterested Being. He is deeply invested in the human story and deeply in love with what He has fashioned. God wants to know and be known by us.

DAY 2

January 2

Genesis 3:1–4:26; Matthew 2:13–3:6;
Psalm 2:1-12; Proverbs 1:7-9

In all the Bible, one of the saddest stories is told in today's reading. "The fall of man," as it is known, reveals the trajectory of the rest of the Bible and the reason for God's invasion of the earth to rescue His creation in the person of Jesus. The depths of this poignant event in human history is revealed in God's heartbreaking question to Adam and Eve: "What have you done?"

In the Garden of Eden God offered the tree of life and prohibited the tree of the knowledge of good and evil. One wonders at the purpose of a prohibited fruit. But this tree gives us an incredible picture of how deeply invested God is in a first-person relationship with us—how much He desires to know and be known by us. True love isn't something that can be faked. Enslavement can shape one's behavior if the consequences are dire enough, but authentic and true love can only be offered freely from the heart and cannot be simulated. Love can't be true if there is no way out. And the tree of the knowledge of good and evil was exactly that.

Adam and Eve chose to eat of it contrary to God's

command with devastating repercussions, and humankind has been ravaged ever since. We traded perfection and true love for knowledge and have attempted to use that knowledge to imitate sovereignty to frightening and terrible results. Humans are invited to live a life of faith—the reality of what we hope for and the evidence of things we cannot see (Hebrews 11:1)—but we often desire to have things our own way even though that might destroy us. We want to choose for ourselves rather than walk the narrow path that leads to life. Throughout history, humankind has worked to remain self-directed, but this has not brought us back to God. The only way to know Him is through faith, trusting in what He has said and provided.

DAY 3

January 3

Genesis 5:1–7:24; Matthew 3:7–4:11;
Psalm 3:1-8; Proverbs 1:10-19

In these first few days and chapters of the Bible we've gained a context for the stories that will begin to unfold before us. Yesterday we learned of mankind's fall from perfection and total intimacy with God. Murder and death entered the human story—things we were never intended to endure.

Today in Genesis, we jump a millennium into the future and see the devastating results. Humankind had become so corrupt that they acted as animals and had only evil intentions. God regretted creating them. To see us so far from our created state of perfection and intimacy grieved His heart (Genesis 6:5-6). But there was one righteous man—Noah. And we see a redemptive thread weaving its way into the story as a reset of the earth comes by way of a great flood.

In today's New Testament reading, we follow Jesus into the wilderness, where Satan challenged Him. While in the wilderness, the evil one tempted Jesus with an invitation to abort His mission and take the easy way by bowing to Satan—echoes of the same trickery put before Adam and

Eve. Jesus was the first perfect person to walk upon the earth since Adam, and the same type of humanity-twisting temptation was put before Him—as it is for each of us. Of course, Jesus, our definitive example, rebuked the evil one and sent him away. There is no doubt that we confront similar temptations every day. And we respond to them either like Adam and Eve or like Jesus. Each of us daily chooses whether to eat of forbidden fruit or to know God by intimately walking with Him in every thought, word, and deed.

DAY 4

January 4

Genesis 8:1–10:32; Matthew 4:12-25;
Psalm 4:1-8; Proverbs 1:20-23

Today in Genesis we watch as the floodwaters recede and Noah and his family once again place their feet on dry ground. Generations are recited, revealing the ways in which the earth's population grew and spread. In Matthew, we see Jesus' earthly ministry begin and the calling together of men who leave everything behind to follow Jesus. We'll get to know them well, for they become the band of brothers who will walk alongside Him throughout His ministry. But we are also greeted with the way the Bible becomes a mirror into our souls and offers an open hand of friendship by giving us practical advice and truth for our days.

"Don't sin by letting anger control you. Think about it overnight and remain silent," the poet-king David tells us (Psalm 4:4). And although we've not yet met him in the Scriptures, David will teach us a lot about ourselves. How often do we simply live reactionary lives, as if life is happening to us rather than the other way around? David gives us compelling advice that echoes across the millennia. We can imagine the immediate effect it would have on our daily lives if we would not be controlled by anger but would allow for silence and perspective. "Come and listen to my counsel. I'll share my heart with you and make you wise," the Proverbs tell us today. May we accept this invitation and make space in our lives for wisdom to guide us (Proverbs 1:23).

Prayer

Lord, I will regard the words of wisdom that You have provided today. The Bible is marvelous in that it allows us to learn in so many ways—through direct teaching and history, through the stories of those who have gone before, through the teaching and humanity of Jesus. As the Proverbs suggest, I will listen to Your counsel, for I want You to share Your heart with me and not just the other way around.

DAY 5

January 5

Genesis 11:1–13:4; Matthew 5:1-26;
Psalm 5:1-12; Proverbs 1:24-28

In our Genesis reading we encounter the construction of a tower and a plan to build it to the heavens as a memorial to those who fashioned it. And again, we see God intervening because humans were never intended to be sovereign unto themselves. It is contrary to our true nature, which is to be intimately connected with God. God confused the language of the people at Babel, and humankind spread across the earth as a result.

In Matthew's Gospel, Jesus begins to teach one of His foundational messages, known as the Sermon on the Mount. This disruptive message describes a world that we long for but have no idea how to achieve. And perhaps that is the entire point. Like the people at the Tower of Babel, we cannot achieve the life we long for through our own cunning and ingenuity. We may accomplish marvelous things, but without a total dependence on God we are completely unable to fill the void within ourselves. Jesus spoke of the countless blessings for those who reach the end of their own strength and ability, only to find God there. We are happiest when we depend on God for everything we are and everything we ever will be.

May we truly depend on God today in every choice we make and word we speak, knowing that we are safe in His care when we live in the light and walk in truth. It's our choice. In the Proverbs today we see that this choice has always been before us: "I called you so often, but you wouldn't come. I reached out to you, but you paid no attention. You ignored my advice and rejected the correction I offered" (Proverbs 1:24-25). These words resonate because we know we've been that person. But this is a new day. May we pay vigilant attention to the voice of Jesus, who gives us the wisdom we need to navigate through our days.

DAY 6

January 6

Genesis 13:5–15:21; Matthew 5:27-28;
Psalm 6:1-10; Proverbs 1:29-33

Yesterday we got a brief introduction to a man named Abram. We'll get to know him much better in the coming days, for it is through him that the faith we freely enjoy finds an anchor.

Eventually his name would become Abraham, and the reverberations of his life echo until today.

God called Abram to a land he had never been in and promised him that the land, as far as he could see in all directions, would one day belong to his family. And from this promise the land would eventually become known as the "Promised Land." The problem was that Abram was getting old and had no children to inherit this land regardless of the promise. God invited him outside and, against the backdrop of an immense sky of stars, told him, "Look up into the sky and count the stars if you can. That's how many descendants you will have!" (Genesis 15:5). Abram had faith in God at that moment, and God considered him righteous because of it. So, the next time you have a moment of uncertainty regarding your faith, go outside to look at the stars and remember God's faithfulness to those who trust Him.

The Proverbs today show us the alternative: "For they hated knowledge and chose not to fear the LORD. They rejected my advice and paid no attention when I corrected them. Therefore, they must eat the bitter fruit of living their own way, choking on their own schemes" (Proverbs 1:29-31). We have a choice in this. We can fall into the overwhelming grace of a loving God by doing nothing more than trusting and intimately walking with Him, or we can choke on our own schemes. This is always the choice before us, but it's not because God is pompous or tyrannical. It's because this is how we were made—to know and be known by God.

DAY 7

January 7

Genesis 16:1–18:15; Matthew 6:1-24;
Psalm 7:1-17; Proverbs 2:1-5

Abraham received a promise from God that his progeny would one day inherit a promised land. But Abraham had no children. This problem is addressed in today's reading. "I will return to you about this time next year, and your wife, Sarah, will have a son," God told Abraham (Genesis 18:10). Abraham's wife, Sarah, overheard this and laughed to herself because she was too old to have children. But God called her out on it and reiterated that she would bear a son.

What have you been holding out hope for in life? What if you were promised, "About this time next year . . ."? Would hope rise? Or have you been laughing at the impossible?

In our New Testament reading, Jesus has much to teach us about the posture of the Kingdom of God. Throughout His life on earth He was the picture of true servanthood. He taught that if you're going to help somebody, don't make a big deal about it by broadcasting your good deeds so that you get the praise and affirmation. If that's what you're after, then you already have your reward. However, if you want to find a correct heart posture, don't even let your left hand know what your right hand is doing. Do it in secret, and your Father, who sees in secret, will give you your reward. It's the same with prayer: Don't be fake and proclaim elaborate and complex prayers so everyone can see how "godly" and "spiritual" you are. Go into your private room, pray to your Father in secret, and He will hear you.

Jesus then takes us into a place that we ignore at our own peril. "If you forgive those who sin against you, your heavenly Father will forgive you. But if you refuse to forgive others, your Father will not forgive your sins" (Matthew 6:14). Forgiveness is not an option in God's Kingdom. But forgiveness does not mean that we pretend things didn't happen. Rather, it means that we have a place to release those people and events in our lives that have sabotaged us for too long. Forgiveness is a command—yes—but it's also an invitation to the emancipation of our souls. When we forgive, we are forgiven.

Prayer

Our Father in heaven, may Your name be kept holy. May Your Kingdom come soon. May Your will be done on earth, as it is in heaven. Give us today the food we need, and forgive us our sins, as we have forgiven those who sin against us. And don't let us yield to temptation, but rescue us from the evil one (Matthew 6:9-13).